POVERTY AND SCHOOLING IN THE U.S.

Contexts and Consequences

Sociocultural, Political, and Historical Studies in Education
Joel Spring, Editor

Spring • The Cultural Transformation of a Native American Family and Its Tribe 1763–1995

Peshkin • Places of Memory: Whiteman's Schools and Native American Communities

Nespor • Tangled Up in School: Politics, Space, Bodies, and Signs in the Educational Process

Weinberg • Asian-American Education: Historical Background and Current Realities

Lipka/Mohatt/The Ciulistet Group • Transforming the Culture of Schools: Yu'pik Eskimo Examples

Benham/Heck • Culture and Educational Policy in Hawai'i: The Silencing of Native Voices

Spring • Education and the Rise of the Global Economy

Pugach • On the Border of Opportunity: Education, Community, and Language at the U.S.-Mexico Line

Hones/Cha • Educating New Americans: Immigrant Lives and Learning

Gabbard, Ed. • Knowledge and Power in the Global Economy: Politics and the Rhetoric of School Reform

Glander • Origins of Mass Communications Research During the American Cold War: Educational Effects and Contemporary Implications

Neito, Ed. • Puerto Rican Students in U.S. Schools

Benham/Cooper, Eds. • Indigenous Educational Models for Contemporary Practice: In Our Mother's Voice

Spring • The Universal Right to Education: Justification, Definition, and Guidelines

Peshkin • Permissible Advantage?: The Moral Consequences of Elite Schooling

DeCarvalho • Rethinking Family–School Relations: A Critique of Parental Involvement in Schooling

Borman/Stringfield/Slavin, Eds. • Title I: Compensatory Education at the Crossroads

Roberts • Remaining and Becoming: Cultural Crosscurrents in an Hispano School

Meyer/Boyd, Eds. • Education Between State, Markets, and Civil Society: Comparative Perspectives

Luke • Globalization and Women in Academics: North/West—South/East

Grant/Lei, Eds. • Global Constructions of Multicultural Education: Theories and Realities

Spring • Globalization and Educational Rights: An Intercivilizational Analysis

Spring • Political Agendas for Education: From the Religious Right to the Green Party, Second Edition

McCarty • A Place to Be Navajo: Rough Rock and The Struggle for Self-Determination in Indigenous Schooling

Hones, Ed. • American Dreams, Global Visions: Dialogic Teacher Research With Refugee and Immigrant Families

Benham/Stein, Eds. • The Renaissance of American Indian Higher Education: Capturing the Dream

Ogbu • Black American Students in an Affluent Suburb: A Study of Academic Disengagement

Books, Ed. • Invisible Children in the Society and Its Schools, Second Edition

Spring • Educating the Consumer-Citizen: A History of the Marriage of Schools, Advertising, and Media

Hemmings • Coming of Age in U.S. High Schools: Economic, Kinship, Religious, and Political Crosscurrents

Heck • Studying Educational and Social Policy: Theoretical Concepts and Research Methods

Lakes/Carter, Eds. • Globalizing Education for Work: Comparative Perspectives on Gender and the New Economy

Spring • How Educational Ideologies are Shaping Global Society: Intergovernmental Organizations, NGOs, and the Decline of the Nation-State

Shapiro/Pupel, Eds. • Critical Social Issues in American Education: Democracy and Meaning in a Globalizing World, Third Edition

Books • Poverty and Schooling in the U.S.: Contexts and Consequences

Reagan • Non-Western Educational Traditions: Alternative Approaches to Educational Thought and Practice, Third Edition

Bowers, Ed. • Rethinking Freire: Globalization and the Environmental Crisis

---

POVERTY AND SCHOOLING IN THE U.S.

Contexts and Consequences

Sue Books

State University of New York at New Paltz

2004

LAWRENCE ERLBAUM ASSOCIATES, PUBLISHERS
Mahwah, New Jersey London

Grateful acknowledgment is made to the following:

The University of Chicago Press for permission to reprint two excerpts from *Lives on the Edge: Single Mothers and Their Children in the Other America*, by Valerie Polakow. Copyright © 1993.

The William Blake Archive for permission to reprint a portion of "The Chimney Sweeper." Copyright © 2003.

Part of Chapter 5 appeared in slightly different form as "Playing with Numbers, Playing with Need: Schooling and the Federal Poverty Line" in *Educational Foundations, 14*(2), 5–20. Copyright © 2000 by Caddo Gap Press. Reprinted with permission.

Part of Chapter 6 appeared in slightly different form as "Funding Accountability: States, Courts, and Public Responsibility" in *Educational Studies, 34*(3), 317–336. Copyright © 2003 by Lawrence Erlbaum Associates, Inc. Reprinted with permission.

Lawrence Erlbaum Associates, Inc., Publishers
10 Industrial Avenue
Mahwah, New Jersey 07430

Cover design by Kathryn Houghtaling Lacey

Library of Congress Cataloging-in-Publication Data

Books, Sue.
Poverty and schooling in the U.S. : contexts and consequences / Sue Books.
p. cm.

Includes bibliographical references and index.
ISBN 0-8058-5193-3 (cloth : alk. paper)
ISBN 0-8058-3893-7 (pbk. : alk. Paper)
1. Poor children—Education—United States. 2. Poor children—United States—Social conditions—21st century. 3. Educational equalization—United States. I. Title: Poverty and schooling in the United States. II. Title.

LC4091.B66 2004
371.826'942'0973—dc22

2004046921
CIP

Books published by Lawrence Erlbaum Associates are printed on acid-free paper, and their bindings are chosen for strength and durability.

Printed in the United States of America
10 9 8 7 6 5 4 3 2 1

To my mother and father, Fred and Teeny Thompson,
with many thanks.

Contents

Preface

This book is in part a plea, especially to colleagues and future colleagues in the profession of education, to undertake the intellectual and emotional work of learning more about the social causes as well as the sometimes life-altering consequences of poverty. Will such efforts eradicate poverty? Almost certainly not. Will they help make us better educators, administrators, policymakers, and researchers—which is to say, more insightful human beings able to discern and respond to the needs of others? I believe they will. I believe efforts to understand the causes and consequences of poverty will help us all gain perspective, make difficult decisions more thoughtfully, and remain truer to that which matters most: the bonds of love and care among people.

This book is also an effort, undertaken in the spirit of a Freirian dialog, to bring to the table of a larger conversation about the educational significance of poverty information about the social policy context of poverty, about typical school experiences of poor children, and about the law-and-policy context of schooling as it affects poor children. Although the long struggle for social justice and equal educational opportunity requires much more than information, good information helps us ask better questions and transcend a dangerous consciousness of "us versus them" that relegates poor children to second-class status.

"Many of the liberal intellectuals I know who are concerned with questions of unequal access to good secondary schools tend to focus more on inequalities that may be caused by our selection systems than on those that are engendered by environmental forces and are neurological in nature," Kozol (1995) writes in *Amazing Grace*. "In human terms, it's understandable that people would prefer to speak about examinations than about brain damage" (p. 156). As Kozol suggests, owning up to the real consequences of poverty is not always easy; nevertheless, educators need to undertake this work.

Because poverty affects children's physical, emotional, and cognitive development, it is an educational issue. Because ideas affect beliefs about what is fair and unfair and affect assumptions about what is inevitable or merely a function of human choice and decision making, education and poverty are linked in a complicated relationship. Along with whatever else schools do, they traffic in ideas. Especially in times such as ours, times challenged by the problems reflected in the statistics cited throughout this book, taken-for-granted ideas about poverty and poor children must be scrutinized and reconsidered. In this task, education remains profoundly relevant.

The chapters that follow build on this argument. Chapter 2 describes what I regard as the informational component of good teaching—that is, what teachers need to know or understand about the contexts and consequences of poverty. Chapters 3 through 5 focus on the situation of poor children outside schools. Chapter 3 provides information about the social context of poverty (post-1996 welfare "reform," wages and job opportunities, economic polarization, and tax cuts and budget crises) and considers the "dependency" not of the poor on the well-to-do, but vice versa. Chapter 4 focuses on the experience of many children and families living in poverty. Chapter 5 documents the demographics of poverty and offers a critique of the official U.S. poverty metric.

Chapters 6 through 9 focus on the situation of poor children inside schools and on the law-and-policy context of educational reform. Chapter 6 reports on continuing and significant disparities in school funding. Chapter 7 provides historical context through a broad-brush review of some of the landmark moments in the legal struggle for equal educational opportunity: *Brown v. Board of Education of Topeka* (1954), which found state-imposed segregation in schooling based on race to be unconstitutional; *San Antonio Independent School District v. Rodriguez* (1973), which found that education is not a fundamental right protected by the U.S. Constitution; and *Milliken v. Bradley* (1974), which blocked efforts to integrate racially isolated city schools through interdistrict, city–suburban remedies in the absence of proof that suburban or state officials contributed directly to segregation. Chapter 8 looks at some typical school experiences of poor children, and Chapter 9 considers the consequences for poor children of the No Child Left Behind Act, the most recent enactment of the Elementary and Secondary Education

Act, signed into law by President George W. Bush, and of other federal education-related initiatives.

The book concludes with thoughts about the kind of educational reform that would make a difference in the lives of poor children—namely, a reform movement driven by a realistic and advocacy-oriented agenda, by a public discourse that owns up to the real consequences of poverty, and by a willingness to eradicate the systemic injustices that reproduce inequalities in social opportunities, including and especially educational opportunities for poor children.

ACKNOWLEDGMENTS

Many people, far too many to name, influenced and supported me as I wrote, and prepared to write, this book. A few, however, shaped my thinking significantly, and I want to thank them by name, without suggesting that they necessarily agree with anything I have written: David Purpel, my mentor as a doctoral student at the University of North Carolina at Greensboro; Valerie Polakow, a brilliant scholar whose intellect is deeply rooted in her outrage and compassion; and my father, the Rev. Fred Thompson, whose lifelong struggle to live in accord with his own moral ideals has shown me both the possibility and the steadfastness required in this most human of challenges.

I thank my new husband, Paul Edlund, for his endless patience and strong support, which enabled me to see this project through; my daughter, Cora, for her love and for the many years we have spent growing together; and my wonderful editor, Naomi Silverman, for her faith in this project long before I could imagine it coming to fruition. I thank Sandra Winn Tutwiler and Kathy Farber for their thoughtful comments on the prospectus for this book; Leslie Bloom, Nirali Parekh, and my colleague Michael Muffs for comments on selected chapters; and Nirali for help with the index. At Lawrence Erlbaum Associates, Inc., Sara Scudder and Erica Kica helped make the book a reality.

Parts of this book revise and expand earlier scholarship. Parts of Chapter 3 build on a chapter in *Kidworld: Childhood Studies, Global Perspectives, and Education*, edited by G. S. Cannella and J. L. Kincheloe (Peter Lang, 2002), "Making Poverty Pay: Children and the 1996 Welfare Law," and on a chapter in *The Public Assault on America's Children: Poverty, Violence, and Juvenile Injustice*, edited by Valerie Polakow (Teachers College Press, 2000), "Poverty and Environmentally Induced Damage to Children." Part of Chapter 8 builds on an article published in 2001 in *Educational Foundations, 15*(4), 57–70, "High Stakes in New York: From a 'Last Chance, First Chance' Classroom," and part of Chapter 10, on a chapter in *Schooling and Standards in the United States: An Encyclopedia*, edited by J. Kincheloe and D. Weil (ABC-CLIO Publishers, 2001), "Saying Poverty Doesn't Matter Doesn't Make It So."

1

Introduction

I hope this book provides educators with a resource for teaching and learning about poverty and its effect on children and families. In writing the book, I have drawn from my experience teaching graduate and undergraduate students in educational foundations courses at the State University of New York at New Paltz. When one of my students, an educator who teaches some of the poorest children in upstate New York, told our class, "I've become able to see my own students differently," she gave me the push I needed to begin the project.

My teaching has led me to few conclusions, however. Always, at the end of the semester, I have been pleased in some ways but not in others with the learning that seemingly has transpired. Consequently, readers hoping for a "how to teach about poverty" book likely will be disappointed.

Instead, I hope the book encourages reflection about the experience of growing up poor in a wealthy society, about a society that tolerates this on a broad scale, and about what this means for teachers and teacher educators. Such reflection likely will lead people in different directions. Some might seek to influence social and educational policy. Others might initiate projects of advocacy within schools. Yet others might quietly reshape their perceptions and, therefore, their pedagogy to create classrooms more welcoming to all students, especially those whose lives have been constrained unnecessarily by the hunger, uncertainty, and distress that come so often with life in poverty. Such reflection is unlikely to lead, however, to study of the poor or to the sadly recurrent question of how best to "fix" poor children (Connell, 1994). What poor children need and deserve, but all too often do not get, are good teaching, good schools, and access to opportunities passed through social networks.

Educational reform efforts focused on the poor historically have drawn on and spurred research that amounts to studying the poor, including and especially their alleged deficiencies. This book starts in a different place. I wrote it in the hope that it would encourage practicing and prospective teachers and teacher educators to consider what's wrong not with the poor, but rather with a social system that provides a wealth of opportunities for some and constraints for others. I hope this book helps educators consider what this system means for poor children, and how they might best respond in and outside their professional roles.

I often have shared this story (origins unknown to me) with my students as a way of illustrating the importance not only of responding to immediate needs, but also of gaining understanding of their causes and consequences:

> Three men walking along a riverbank noticed children in the river, floundering and struggling as if they were drowning. Two of the three jumped in and pulled the children out—one, then another, then another. The third man wandered upstream. The first two rescued all the children without the help of their friend, who finally came back.
>
> "Where were you?" they asked in exasperation. "We needed help!"
>
> "I know," the third man replied, "but somebody needed to find out who was throwing all the children in the water."

Teachers must respond with competence and compassion to "drowning" children. Yet teachers also need to understand why so many children are in this situation to start with and to know more than many do about their students and the broader social/cultural context of their lives.

I will not be surprised if some readers find this book lacking in that it fails to provide "answers." This would be a fair observation, and perhaps a fair critique. I have not tried to provide a solution to "the problem of poverty" because I believe this is far beyond the powers of individual educators or even the profession of education. Significantly reducing poverty will require abolishing ghettos, providing all workers with a living wage, and allowing parents and other caregivers to devote adequate time to childrearing. At the same time, although teachers cannot "cure" poverty by themselves, they can—indeed, cannot help but—respond to the poverty that walks into their classrooms in the minds and bodies of millions of children. Pubic schools are sometimes the safest place many students ever will be, places where children potentially can eat breakfast and lunch, see a nurse, and encounter adults who treat them as "children of promise" (Swadener & Lubeck, 1995) whose intellectual lives and personal development matter tremendously.

In some ways, I have been writing this book most of my life. I grew up in a middle-class family in Charlotte, North Carolina, where both my parents also were raised, albeit in much different circumstances. Poverty was something they both had known and wanted me not to experience. Long before I acquired a vocabulary of social class, I understood it emotionally. In the early 1980s, as a divorced single mother with a very young daughter, I lived on the edge of poverty for several years, although with a safety net in the form of a mother, father, and sister willing to help, as well as a master's degree and 10 years' experience in the fields of journalism and publishing. Many people helped make those years less difficult than they might have been—most of all, my lovely, vibrant daughter. Still, the experience affected me deeply.

When I moved with my young daughter from Pennsylvania to North Carolina in the early 1980s, I encountered landlords who did not want to rent to someone with a child, prospective employers who worried that I would miss too much work as a single mother, and a doctor who refused to continue seeing my daughter when we joined the ranks of the uninsured. Yet, I recall clearly the day at a public health clinic when a receptionist grilled an African-American woman standing next to me about her relationship with her child's father while questioning me only about relevant matters, such as what immunizations my daughter had had and when. I recall also the day a worker in the county child-support system told me her full-time job paid less than my graduate teaching assistantship and part-time work as a courier for a travel agency.

Those years drove home to me the social foundations of identity. In my own eyes, I was the same person when I arrived in North Carolina as an unemployed single mother that I had been in Pennsylvania as a news reporter and wife. Yet I felt the shift as, in other people's eyes, I inched toward "them" and away from "us." I felt myself become, in the eyes of others, a problem.

As perhaps is already clear, this book has a point of view. I believe people in this country without much money are exploited, treated as second-class citizens, and deprived of many of their rights, and I hope this book provokes more outrage, especially among educators, about this social injustice and its educational significance. As Purpel and Shapiro (1995) argue:

> To know without a sense of outrage, compassion, or concern deadens our souls and significantly eases the struggle of demonic forces to capture our consciousness. We need an education that produces moral indignation and energy rather than one that excuses, mitigates, and temporizes human misery (p. 156).

Reflecting on poverty and schooling brings us face to face with injustice, exploitation, and our own implication in all that has been lost, all that is now being lost. Owning up to this can be difficult work, fraught with the temptations of denial, evasion, and blame. Such honesty also can be empowering. We live not by incentives, whether carrots or sticks, but rather by the ideals and commitments that give our lives meaning and purpose.

When we offer a curriculum that skirts, downplays, or trivializes the moral weight of the glaring injustices of our time—unnecessary hunger, homelessness, and poverty; the ghettoization of entire communities; exploitation of the poor and the vulnerable for profit or sport—we encourage students to regard their time in school as no more than a series of hoops to jump, to gain a reward or avoid punishment (Kohn, 1999). Instead, education ought to push in the opposite direction by helping us to affirm ideals and strengthen commitments through ever deeper and more generous perceptions of the lives and relationships that make up our shared world.

2

What Teachers Need to Know About Poverty

> *We have yet to grapple with what knowledge does to teachers, particularly, the difficult knowledge of social catastrophe, evidence of woeful disregard, experiences of social violence, illness, and death, and most generally, with what it means to come to terms with various kinds of trauma, both individual and collective.*
>
> —*Britzman (2000, pp. 200–205)*

Poor children bear the brunt of almost every imaginable social ill. In disproportionate numbers, they suffer hunger and homelessness; untreated sickness and chronic conditions such as asthma, ear infections, and tooth decay; lead poisoning and other forms of environmental pollution; and a sometimes debilitating level of distress created by crowded, run-down living spaces, family incomes that fall far short of family needs, and ongoing threats of street violence and family dissolution. These same children are assigned, again in skewed numbers, to the nation's worst public schools—schools in the worst states of disrepair and with the lowest levels of per-pupil funding. Not surprisingly, therefore, poor children as a group lag far behind others in educational achievement.

I start with these facts because the social horror of poverty and injustice, two sides of the same coin, is so often overlooked or discounted, as if it doesn't really matter. Yes, I can imagine someone saying, some do get more than others, but whoever said life was fair? And what about the significance of personal initiative and the courage to "go for one's dreams?" Certainly, luck, talent, and determination figure into the winding path any person's life takes. This book is not about that, however, but rather about the social, and especially the educational, significance of poverty. Many children who grow up in poverty thrive despite tremendous hardships. This testifies to the amazing strength of their young spirits, but cannot, or ought not, be used as a reason to deny the profound significance of poverty in young lives. That some children flourish despite the poverty they suffer is a credit to them, not a justification for nonchalance in the face of socially induced hardship. Blake's (1789/2003) young chimney sweep of the 18th century spoke prophetically to one of the horrors of our time too:

> And because I am happy and dance and sing,
>
> They think they have done me no injury.
>
> And are gone to praise God and his Priest and King
>
> Who make up a heaven of our misery.

That many poor children "dance and sing" does not make child poverty not so bad after all. Rather, it underscores how much is destroyed when a growing "social toxicity" (Vorrasi & Garbarino, 2000) suffused by poverty is either rationalized as inevitable or ignored because it is regarded as unimportant.

Teachers obviously cannot eliminate poverty single-handedly. They cannot reconfigure the nation's political economy or redraw its social landscape. They cannot reshape the job market or change social policies governing housing and health care. At the same time, teachers can—and inevitably do—*respond* to the injustice to which poor children bear such painful witness. Consider, for example, the compassion and understanding Polakow (1993) observed in a kindergarten classroom, taught by Ms. Juno. Six-year-old Carrie often came to school distraught. Quick to pick fights with classmates, she was slow to join group activities. On this day:

> The children sit on the rug and listen to the story "The Very Hungry Caterpillar." All are in the circle except Carrie, who sits at the arts and crafts table cutting paper. "Ms. Juno, Carrie's not in the circle," says one little girl. "I know," replies Ms. Juno, "she'll come when she's ready." When the story is over, Ms. Juno announces she has a surprise. She goes into the closet and emerges with a large tank filled with sand. "Guess what I have in here." "A caterpillar," says Travis. "Right," replies Ms. Juno, "all sorts of worms and caterpillars." In twos the children take turns at the tank and fish out worms and caterpillars. Carrie, after watching from her vantage point at the table, slowly edges closer until she is in the circle. Ms. Juno calls her up together with Annie, a

> child who sometimes plays with Carrie. After the hands-on caterpillar activity, the children are given a choice of painting, drawing, or writing a story about caterpillars. Carrie chooses painting and goes straight to the easel; with deep concentration she spends almost fifteen minutes painting a picture of a "caterpillar family" and then counting all their legs. (pp. 135–136)

Later:

> During small group time, when Carrie is sitting next to Pat, she takes his colored marker and pokes him. Pat moves away, saying, "I wish I didn't have sat next to you." Carrie tries to write on his shirt with the marker. Pat shouts, "Quit it," and calls, "Ms. Juno, Ms. Juno, Carrie's writing on my shirt." Ms. Juno comes over and moves Carrie, saying, "Carrie, you cannot write on people's shirts, that really makes Pat feel bad—now come over here with me by my table." Carrie goes to Ms. Juno and pleads with her tearfully, "Don't tell my mother, she got sick again in the hospital." "Your mother will be real pleased to hear how well you've been doing, Carrie. Yesterday you were real helpful, and today's been hard for you, but we'll work on it." (Polakow, 1993, p. 136)

Carrie and her two siblings live in a subsidized apartment with their mother, who has been hospitalized twice with a serious illness. Since Carrie's mother lost a part-time job due to illness, the family has lived in "constant crisis," her teacher said, and has struggled to survive on public assistance through periods of eviction and a temporary cutoff of Medicaid insurance. When Carrie becomes aggressive with classmates, Ms. Juno pulls her away from the situation, gives her time to calm down, then works with all the children to help them understand each other's feelings. "Carrie is worried about her mommy and sometimes she feels sad or mad because she's going through a hard time, and we all need to help her," she told the children in the class (Polakow, 1993, p. 137). Some of Carrie's classmates avoid her, but others seek her out and try to make her feel better.

Like all classroom interactions, this one is complex. Yet it suggests the role of basic understanding in shaping teacher–student relationships. Carrie's teacher, Ms. Juno, knows something about the enormous stress in Carrie's life and responds with warmth, compassion, and the flexibility she believes Carrie needs to find a place for herself in the classroom. Over the course of her observations, Polakow (1993) saw some progress—no miracles, but signs of growing confidence and participation. "I can read real books now," Carrie told a friend enthusiastically. "Ms. Juno said I get to read my book I made to the whole class in circle time" (p. 138).[1]

After many years of observing "star teachers of children in poverty," Haberman (1995) concluded that these teachers' judgments and actions in the classroom reflect deep-seated beliefs about teaching, learning, and children. Consequently, Haberman (1995) offers not "10 easy steps" to becoming a star teacher, but rather a discussion of some of the commitments and beliefs evident in classrooms in which poor children flourish. One such belief is recognition that challenges come with the territory of teaching. "Star" teachers

> begin each semester knowing they will teach some youngsters who are affected by handicapping conditions. They anticipate that horrendous home, poverty, and environmental conditions will impinge on their students. They know that inadequate health care and nutrition, and various forms of substance and physical abuse, typify the daily existence of many of their students. In short, stars assume that the reason youngsters need teachers is because there will be all manner of serious interferences with their teaching and with students' learning. (Haberman, 1995, p. 3)

"Because they do not regard their students as animals to be shaped," star teachers are not preoccupied with rewards and punishments (Haberman, 1995, p. 7). Because they do not regard poor families as scapegoats, they use what they know about their students and their families as a basis for helping students learn, never as fodder for parent bashing. Star teachers recognize that "most parents care a great deal and, if approached in terms of what they can do, will be active, cooperative partners" (Haberman, 1995, p. 12).

These teachers see their fundamental task as engaging students in educationally worthwhile activities and consequently "evaluate themselves whenever they assess student performance" (Haberman, 1995, p. 12). If students seem disengaged, star teachers wonder what they might do differently, and try something new—again and again, if necessary. These teachers *persist*, not because of an irrational faith in their students, not because they regard themselves as heroes, and not because they are determined to have their way. Rather, their persistence "re-

---

[1]Polakow (1993) observed Carrie during the course of a broader research project that documents the classroom worlds of poor children. As Section III of her book *Lives on the Edge: Single Mothers and Their Children in the Other America* shows, Carrie's experience of compassion and understanding contrasts sharply with the demeaning treatment many other poor children receive.

veals the deep and abiding beliefs that stars hold about the nature of children in poverty and their potential; the nature of stars' roles as teachers; and the reasons stars believe they and the children are in school"—namely, for children to learn about themselves and their world (Haberman, 1995, p. 21).

All teachers need the kind of understanding evident in Ms. Juno's response to Carrie as well as the commitment and persistence Haberman (1995) praises. Such a foundation cannot be reduced to the acquisition of information. At the same time, although knowing more does not guarantee better practice, knowing something about poverty gives teachers a place to start.

Such a foundation would include the recognition that poverty is a function of political economy, not of scarcity and not of personality. In wealthy nations such as the United States where there is no absolute scarcity of food, shelter, health care, or opportunity, poverty results from the politics of distribution. Although statistics justify the popular observation that "the rich get richer and the poor get poorer," politics drives this distributive trend, not natural law and not personal traits. Laziness, promiscuity, poor judgment, devaluation of education—none of these popular assumptions about the poor are either unique to any socioeconomic group or a cause of poverty in any demonstrable sense. Poor people do not cause poverty any more than enslaved human beings caused a system of institutionalized slavery to thrive in this country (Chamberlin, 1999), and just as studying the behavior or beliefs of slaves will not provide insight into institutionalized slavery, scrutinizing the behavior or beliefs of impoverished people will not lead to an understanding of how and why poverty persists in the United States.

Second, teachers need to recognize that poverty is not a Black problem, an immigrant problem, a single-mother problem, or a "don't want to work" problem. Statistics do not back up this picture of poverty and its causes. As chapter 5 documents, most people living in poverty are White, most live outside central cities (many in isolated rural areas), and about half of all poor families are headed by two parents or by single fathers. It is also the case that people of color, people living in central cities, and single-mother families are poor in disproportionate numbers. Both realities are important. Recognizing the scope of poverty and its prevalence among people of all racial and ethnic groups, in all family configurations, and in all geographic areas mediates against notions of the poor as "them"—those "others" who in some essential way, many people imagine, are not at all like themselves (Katz, 1989).

At the same time, recognizing how widely (disproportionately) poverty is suffered by people of color, especially by young children in single-mother families in central cities, leads, or ought to lead, to questions about the role of racism and sexism in perpetuating destitution.

An emotionally charged public discourse props up a host of theories about the causes of poverty: single motherhood, lack of a work ethic, failure to accept personal responsibility or to "find" a job, and "dependency," the alleged personality flaw behind the need for public assistance. None of this stands up under the light of serious inquiry. As just one example, consider a comparative study of child poverty in 23 wealthy nations by the United Nations Children's Fund Innocenti Research Centre (2000a). The study found that neither the percentage of children living in single-parent families nor a nation's rate of joblessness correlated very closely with its rate of child poverty.[2] The percentage of children living in single-parent families varies greatly across the nations, from less than 1% in Turkey to more than 20% in Sweden, but these percentages bear little relationship to rates of child poverty. Proportionally, more children live in single-parent families in Sweden than in the United States, yet the child poverty rate in Sweden is one tenth the rate of child poverty in this country. Almost the same percentage of children live in single-parent families in Canada as in Finland, but the child poverty rate in Canada is more than three times as high as the rate in Finland. Although children in single-parent families are much more likely to grow up in poverty than children in two-parent families, at least in the United States, this cross-nation comparison suggests the need to look beyond single motherhood as a *cause* of poverty. When strong social supports for families and decent job opportunities are available, single-mother families are far less likely to live in poverty.

The Innocenti researchers also found no clear-cut relationship between rates of unemployment and of child poverty across the 23 nations. Spain and Japan have widely differing rates of joblessness but about the same level of child poverty. The United States and Mexico have relatively low levels of unemployment, but relatively high levels of child poverty. In Finland, the reverse is true. Critical factors, of course, are wages and the distribution of job opportunities. If wages are

[2]The study, based largely on analysis of the household data sets in the Luxembourg Income Study, used a relative measure of child poverty: a family income below half the median in the nation. Poverty rates, depending on the country, refer to the years 1990 through 1997.

too low, jobs do not lift families out of poverty, and if jobs that pay a living wage go primarily to members of households already living comfortably, they do little to alter a nation's child poverty rate.

Welfare reformers in the United States trumpeted the 1996 repeal of the 60-year-old federal guarantee of support for poor families as a much-needed crack-down on the alleged problem of "dependency," to which poor mothers presumably had fallen victim. Faced with the choice of finding a job or accepting a "handout," the story went, poor mothers in droves opted not to work. In fact, welfare benefits had been dropping for decades prior to the passage of the Personal Responsibility and Work Opportunity Act of 1996 and never brought families up even to the official poverty line. Far from enabling poor families to live comfortably, the maligned Aid to Families with Dependent Children (AFDC) program never enabled poor mothers even to meet basic family needs. Furthermore, a corresponding drop in the rate of child poverty has not accompanied the precipitous drop in the welfare rolls of almost 60% between 1996 and 2002.

With very few exceptions, work is now the law of the land, but this has not changed the lot of millions of children still living in poverty and in many cases has made it worse. The Economic Policy Institute (Boushey, Brocht, Gundersen, & Bernstein, 2001) estimates that almost 30% of families with one to three children under 12 have incomes too small to meet basic family needs, and that half of these families include an adult who works. In 1999, most poor children (78%) lived in a family in which someone worked at least part of the year (Children's Defense Fund, 2001a).

In addition to gaining some understanding of the causes and consequences of poverty, teachers need to recognize that almost all parents and caregivers, regardless of family income, want the best for their children and care about their education. Without the respect grounded in this recognition, teachers and school administrators cannot develop constructive relationships with families and communities. It has been said so often it now seems accepted as truth that parents in poor communities "don't care" about education. Neither research nor the experience of school leaders supports this presumption (Haberman, 1995; Lareau, 1989). "All parents want the best for their children. I've had crack-addicted mothers in my office demanding the best for their children," the principal of a high-poverty elementary school in Yonkers, New York, told me. "Parents want their kids to do well in school. With whatever they can bring to this world to make that happen, they're doing it," another Yonkers principal observed."[3]

Finally, teachers need to recognize that in schooling, as in society, poverty matters. Paul Houston, executive director of the American Association of School Administrators, makes the point well: "I don't think there's an educator who wouldn't stand up and say, 'Poor kids have more problems when they come to school than kids who come from homes where they're not poor'" (quoted in Hayden & Cauthen, 1998). Study after study, at least since the Coleman (1966) report, has confirmed the significance of poverty in schooling.

At the same time, although poverty matters in schooling, it is not all that matters. In the words of New York State Supreme Court Justice Leland DeGrasse, who overturned New York's highly inequitable system of funding public schools in 2001, "Demography is not destiny" (*Campaign for Fiscal Equity v. State of New York*, 2001). Poverty does not render children uneducable. Yet the school experience of many poor children hinders them more than it helps. This is what needs to change.

In 2001, more than 16% of all children in the United States lived in poverty, according to official calculations. (These statistics are based on an absolute rather than a relative measure of poverty. See chap. 5 for more discussion of this metric and its shortcomings.) The poverty rate for children of color is almost three times as high as the rate for White children. In many of our major cities and rural areas, entire communities are completely impoverished (Chatterley & Rouveral, 2000; Jargowsky, 1997; Kozol, 1995; Shirk, Bennett, & Aber, 1999). In such a society, teachers and teacher educators need to understand something about why poverty persists and how it affects young people. On one hand, this seems like an obvious point, hardly worth making: Teachers need to know something about their students' lives and about the broader social/cultural context of those lives. On the other hand, however, few teacher-education programs require any systematic study of poverty or its consequences for children.

As a foundation of compassion, caring, and empathy, understanding is a prerequisite for good teaching (Martin, 1992; Noddings, 1992;

---

[3]During the summer of 1999, I interviewed nine principals and assistant principals in seven high-poverty schools in upstate New York about how poverty affects schooling, in general as well as in their own work. In all but one of the schools, most of the students were eligible to receive subsidized lunches, a commonly used index of poverty. For a fuller analysis, see Books (2001).

Valenzuela, 1999)—a necessary condition, if nevertheless insufficient in and of itself. And understanding comes, of course, not from affirmation of preexisting prejudices (prejudgments) or of media-hyped stereotypes, but rather, at least in part, from a concerted effort to learn, undertaken with openness to the possibility of being challenged and changed. As Greene (1988) argues passionately, insight can make claims on one's life. Coming to understand something in a new way can leave us with no choice but to change our lives, including our professional lives, in response.

I hope this book gives teachers and teacher educators, including myself, a deeper understanding of the significance of poverty in the work of teaching and learning. What any of us do with that knowledge is up to us. What we cannot do, however, is pull ourselves out of the equation. Poverty walks into the classroom in the minds and bodies of children, and we respond—with ignorance or understanding, with hostility or affection, by refusing to acknowledge the toll poverty takes or by throwing our weight into the long struggle for social justice and for the equality in educational opportunity that that struggle has promised but not yet delivered.

The next chapter provides information about the social context of poverty, including welfare "reform," wages and job opportunities, economic polarization, tax cuts, and budget crises in states across the nation. The chapter also offers a view of social relationships that challenges the popular depiction of the poor as dependent.

3

Social Context of Poverty

> *The fundamental problem for the poor in our country is not homelessness or AIDS or hunger or the like—or even any combination of these. They are just symptoms; the problem is injustice ... the inevitable result of the structures of our society—economic, governmental, social, and religious—that undergird inequality. The way things stand now, poverty is built into these systems.*
>
> *—Hilfiker (2000)*

> *To be a member of the working poor is to be an anonymous donor, a nameless benefactor, to everyone else.*
>
> *—Ehrenreich (2001, p. 221)*

The line "You always have the poor with you" is one that "should simply never have made it into the Bible," a Quaker pastor and friend used to say. This book begins with that conviction. Poverty need not be at all, at least not in this richest nation on earth.

> [Poverty] results because some people receive a great deal less than others. Descriptions of the demography, behavior, or beliefs of subpopulations cannot explain the patterned inequalities evident in every era of American history. These result from the styles of dominance, the way power is exercised, and the politics of distribution. (Katz, 1989, p. 7)

There is no absolute scarcity in our society of food, housing, educational opportunity, or work worthy of adequate pay. Poverty arises because of the way these social goods and opportunities are distributed—that is, from the politics of who gets what. Poverty is created and sustained, lessened or made worse, by a myriad of human decisions institutionalized in social policies and practices. There is nothing foreordained about it.

Nevertheless, although poverty need not be "with us," it is. In 2001, 16.3% of all children were poor, based on the official definition: a two-parent family of four with an annual income of no more than $17,960. Many of these children were "extremely poor," meaning their families had annual incomes of less than half the federal poverty line.

These statistics are based on U.S. Census Bureau numbers, which almost certainly distort the scope of economic deprivation and hardship in the United States. The official poverty metric has evolved only slightly from calculations in 1955 of the bare-minimum cost of feeding a family. Few scholars today regard it as a meaningful measure of the income required to live decently in this society (Citro & Michael, 1995). In most parts of the country, a family would need an income roughly double the official poverty line to be able to pay for basic necessities such as food and housing. The National Center for Children in Poverty (Lu, 2003) estimates that 38% of all children live in "low income" families, defined as families with incomes of no more than 200% of the official poverty threshold. This includes 57% of all African-American children, 64% of all Latino children, and 34% of all White children.

According to a report by the U.S. Conference of Mayors (2002), mayors in 25 cities said that hunger and homelessness rose sharply during 2002. Requests for emergency food assistance were up an average of 19%. In 18 cities, requests for emergency shelter were also up 19%. Just over half the mayors said their cities were unable to meet requests for food. The 2002 increases came on top of similarly large jumps the year before—a 23% increase in requests for emergency food assistance and a 13% increase in requests for emergency shelter in 27 cities surveyed.

The desperation these numbers reflect is a function of politics and human-driven economics, not nature. Let me begin, therefore, with a broad-brush overview of the social and political context of poverty in the United States in the early years of the 21st century.

WELFARE "REFORM"

The "end of welfare as we know it"—promised by former President Clinton, accomplished through the Personal Responsibility and Work Opportunity Reconciliation Act of 1996, and embraced with fervor by the Bush Administration—has affected poor women and children profoundly. With this legislation, the nation abolished its 60-year-old guarantee of federal support for the poorest families, restricted assistance for most people to 5 years in a lifetime, gave states lump sums of money to distribute themselves as well as wide discretion to cull people from the welfare rolls, and made assistance contingent with few exceptions on a parent working for wages. Prefaced with a long discussion of the benefits of marriage, studded with statistics used to suggest a causal relationship between single motherhood and poverty, the legislation replaced Aid to Families with Dependent Children (AFDC) with a much different program, Temporary Assistance to Needy Families (TANF), with state control and strict work requirements. Poor mothers now have essentially two choices: marry someone willing and able to support a family or work full-time, regardless of the pay and of the consequences for children.

Not surprisingly, welfare rolls plummeted, 59% between 1996 and 2002—a drop widely heralded as success (Pear, 2003c). But success by what measure? Child poverty also declined during these years, from 20.5% in 1996 to 16.3% in 2001, significantly less than the decrease in the number of families receiving assistance, despite the long stretch of economic prosperity during these years. Despite the overall decrease in child poverty, the rate of extreme poverty among children of all races increased between 1996 and 2001, from 3.6% to 4%. This average includes a sharp jump in the rate among African-American children from 6.4% to 8.4% (Children's Defense Fund, 2003). "The story of deepening poverty is central to the story of Black children in poverty in the wake of the 1996 welfare law," the Children's Defense Fund (2003) warned. "Without it, the story is incomplete."

The Institute for Women's Policy Research (Lyter, Sills, & Oh, 2002) found that family income declined significantly between 1996 and 2000 for extremely poor single-mother families, even though the percentage of these mothers in the workforce increased. Monthly income in extremely poor single-mother families with young children (under 6) dropped from $380 to $301; in similar families with school-aged children, income dropped from $419 to $379. In another assessment of welfare reform, child health researchers (Cook et al., 2002) compared risks of hospitalization and "food insecurity" for infants and toddlers in families receiving public assistance and in families whose benefits had been reduced or terminated due to changes in family income or expenses or failure to comply with welfare rules. The researchers found a 30% higher risk of hospitalization overall, a 90% higher risk of hospitalization at the time of an emergency room visit, and a 50% higher risk of "food insecurity" among children in families that had lost some or all of their welfare benefits. "As child health professionals we are deeply troubled," said Deborah Frank, a principal investigator, who characterized the findings as "an urgent alarm about the unintended effects of welfare reform" (quoted in Boston Medical Center, 2002).

No one knows exactly what has become of all the families formerly receiving welfare benefits. The federal legislation includes no provision for monitoring their post-"reform" condition. Indications are that some have steady jobs with decent pay and benefits, but most are working in low-skill jobs that pay poverty-level wages and offer little security. Single mothers were hit especially hard in 2001 when more than 2 million people across the nation lost their jobs and in many cases were unable to file for unemployment benefits because their jobs were temporary or part-time. About 70% of former welfare recipients who lost jobs during the recession were unable to collect unemployment benefits (Ehrenreich & Piven, 2002).

It is unclear where, if anywhere, these mothers and families can turn for help. After talking with former AFDC recipients in New York, Oregon, California, Florida, and Illinois, Ehrenreich and Piven (2002) concluded:

> [A] maze of obstacles ... now lies between a needy family and even a paltry amount of cash assistance—a set of hurdles far more daunting than the pre-reform bureaucracy. There are long lines in welfare centers with waits, one New York woman told us, of up to nine hours. In a Latino neighborhood, there may be no Spanish-speaking caseworker on duty. In the 1960s, a federal regulation required that welfare offices accept oral applications. Now, you may have to fill out the same form three times, just to save the agency photocopying expenses. (p. 37)

Confronted with this level of discouragement, many people undoubtedly just give up.

A review of studies in 26 states (Richer, Savner, & Greenberg, 2001) found most former welfare recipients were earning $8 an hour or less and a significant share lacked health insurance. Another study found half of former recipients have been unable to buy food for themselves or their children, to pay for utilities, or to maintain regular phone service. One tenth, unable to pay the rent, have been evicted or become homeless (MacKinnon, 2002). The mayor of New York City, faced with a 25% increase in one year in the number of homeless families applying for shelter, sent a group to an unused jail in the Bronx (Steinhauer, 2002).

Economists at the University of California and the Rand Corporation found an increase in the number of children, particularly African-American children in cities, living with relatives or friends, in foster families, or in other arrangements without their mothers or fathers. The study (cited in Bernstein, 2002) found more than 16% of the African-American children in central cities living in such "no-parent households," a percentage that has doubled since the AFDC program was abolished. The increase in children in no-parent households coincides with a decrease in the number in single-parent families.

Without a safety net, many poor mothers face an untenable dilemma: enter into a relationship, any relationship, that promises short-term financial support, or "find" and hold onto a job, whatever this means for children in the absence of suitable child care. Elizabeth Jones, a 26-year-old single mother of three, is in many ways a welfare success story. At the same time, her story, told by Boo (2001), highlights what, at best, might be considered the complexity of welfare reform. The Jones family—Elizabeth, 10-year-old Dernard, 11-year-old Drenika, and 13-year-old Wayne—lives in a neighborhood of 10,000 people in the District of Columbia known as the Shrimp Boat. In 2000, four years after the Personal Responsibility and Work Opportunity Reconciliation Act was passed, Elizabeth had been on welfare for 9 years. After doing some volunteer work and taking a course in word processing, she got a job as a receptionist. A few years later, she graduated from a police academy and started working the night shift in Southeast DC—"the city's most violent quadrant—her own" (Boo, 2001, p. 94). Elizabeth also took a second, part-time job as a security guard.

The two jobs give her an income of about $39,000 a year—an "astronomical sum" compared with the average income of former welfare recipients in Washington, DC ($17,000, according to an Urban Institute study), but nevertheless not enough to meet the basic needs of a family of four ($52,000 a year in DC, according to another study) (Boo, 2001, p. 94). Elizabeth's $1,600-a-month take-home pay from the police department covers the rent and payments on a student loan she took out years ago for a fly-by-night trade school. Wages from the security job go to a car payment and other expenses. Elizabeth has tried repeatedly to collect the child support ($190 a month) she is owed, but with little success. Although she can pay the bills, her life is grueling:

> When her police shift ends, at 4 a.m., she sleeps for two hours, wakes her children for three different schools, sees one to the bus and drives the two others, along with four neighborhood kids who depend on her, to their schools. Then she heads downtown to her part-time job as a private security guard. When she finishes, at 5 p.m., she fetches her children and the four others from their schools, drops them all at their doors, and goes to the police station to start her shift. On days off, she sleeps. (Boo, 2001, p. 97)

Elizabeth worries constantly about her children, especially Drenika. To try to keep her interested in school, Elizabeth petitioned school authorities to transfer Drenika from a troubled school in the Shrimp Boat to another school, five stops away on the bus line, with a principal with an excellent reputation. However, by the time Drenika was enrolled, the principal had taken another job. Because the school often searched in vain for substitute teachers, Drenika spent many hours at school doing nothing. For a variety of reasons, including a shortage of lockers, students were not allowed to take books home.

For Dernard, who in third grade was reading at a seventh-grade level, Elizabeth chose a charter school in the area, which proved to be even worse than Drenika's school. Boo (2001) reports the incident that was the last straw. Elizabeth pulled Dernard out of the school near the end of his fourth-grade year after this day:

> In his classroom, ten boys in khakis and maroon polo shirts sat quietly at empty desks. No books, no paper, not even an objective on the blackboard. They stared into space as the teacher sat at his desk doing the same. Elizabeth grabbed Dernard's books, jumped in her Suzuki, and drove maniacally, the air thick with her undetonated anger. "It's like people think that in this part of town we settle for anything," she said.
>
> "I learned," Dernard said later, trying to make her feel better. "I just learned what I learned already."
>
> Elizabeth did not feel better. (p. 100)

Wayne, Elizabeth's oldest child, artistically talented and learning disabled, languished in regular education classes for years until she found a nonprofit agency that would test him free of charge. Wayne spent his third-, fourth-, and fifth-grade years in a special-education classroom before Elizabeth found a lawyer who, pro bono, pushed the school to review his case. Diagnosed with pervasive developmental disorders, Wayne subsequently was allowed to transfer to a small private high school for disabled children in a Maryland suburb.

Drenika, the middle child, has been taking care of her brothers while her mother works since she was 7 years old. A day-care subsidy Elizabeth received was stopped because of a municipal error, and this seemed like the best plan, all things considered, including the quality of child care Elizabeth could afford. When Drenika started skipping track practice to meet a boy who had been calling her, Elizabeth begged for a work schedule that would allow her to be home in the evenings. "She persuaded her superiors to give her the 11:30 p.m. to 6:30 a.m. shift, which is already overpeopled with single mothers trading sleep and safety for evenings with their children. After a brief reprieve, though, she was returned to 7:30 p.m. to 4 a.m. duty. She got her first gray hair and didn't pluck it—'This one's yours,' she told Drenika" (Boo, 2001, p. 105).

Elizabeth's story invites broader reflection on what welfare "reform" has meant for poor mothers and children. As Boo (2001) points out, "Elizabeth has done everything that reformers could reasonably ask of the daughter of a single mother and a father she never met who, by the age of 21, had a high-school diploma, a history of victimization by rape and domestic abuse, and three babies by three hit-and-run men" (p. 94). By most measures, Elizabeth would be considered an unqualified success. Yet she herself wonders about the "choice" she has made. Had she not left welfare (which actually was not a choice), she suspects she would not have the clarity she has now about what she wants for her children—for them to finish high school and go to college before having children of their own. Yet, she might have more time to help them reach those goals. She suspects "she would have been a better day-to-day mom but a lousier role model, particularly for Drenika" (Boo, 2001, p. 107).

> "Still," she said one day, "it's too hard to think sometimes about a life where I could have real time with Wayne, to read and really help him with things. You can't just schedule him in for half an hour in between jobs, the way I have to do now—he just doesn't work that way. There'd be time to help them all with homework, answer Dernard's million and two questions, do family things—like make a meal together, me and Drenika, instead of calling her in for a catch-up conversation when I'm taking a shower." (Boo, 2001, p. 107)

Boo (2001) shares her own observations: "The exodus of mothers into the workplace has created something new ... a world of free-range children at the mercy of unreformed institutions that, in the absence of parents, are all they have" (p. 95). Studies in three welfare-to-work programs that were precursors to the 1996 welfare overhaul confirm these fears. In all three cases, adolescents with parents participating in the programs had more academic and behavioral problems than adolescents in families receiving public assistance—perhaps, researchers speculated, because parents had less time and energy to monitor young people's activities, including homework, or because much of the responsibility for caring for younger siblings and household chores fell to teenagers (Brooks, Hair, & Zaslow, 2001).

The welfare legislation was up for reauthorization in 2002, but Congress was unable to agree on a bill, so it came up again the next year. The proposal backed by the Bush Administration called for pushing more poor mothers into the workforce and requiring them to work more hours per week. The proposal called for all states, by 2007, to have at least 70% of all welfare recipients, including single mothers with small children, working at least 40 hours a week, which is approximately 6 hours a week more than the national average for working mothers with young children. The plan included no new funds for child care, despite the fact that at the time only one in every seven children eligible for federal child-care assistance was receiving it, and no new funds for transportation and other work-related costs. To many people, this looked like a prescription for more poverty, with little way out for poor mothers and children. The 1996 legislation limited welfare recipients to 1 year of job training; the 2002 proposal called for scaling this back to 3 months, which would rule out not only serious training programs that might prepare people for long-term employment at a living wage, but also substance-abuse treatment.

JOBS AND WAGES

Although the welfare overhaul was never marketed as an antipoverty initiative, it was presented as a way not just to save a few tax dollars, but also to improve the lives of poor women and children. Work would cultivate (by requiring) "personal responsibility" and would enable (by forcing) mothers to become "self-sufficient" and therefore not "dependent." This presumes, however, that those who work are not poor, and this increasingly is not the case. America's Second Harvest (2003), a hunger-relief organization that operates through a national network of food banks, reports that almost 15 million people in the United States are members of working poor families. In 39% of households that rely on soup kitchens, food pantries, and emergency shelters, at least one adults works. Thirty-seven percent of people who request emergency food supplies have jobs, and 70% of poor families include someone who works. Over the past two decades, the poverty rate among working families has increased by almost 50%.

Antipoverty workers have began to speak of the "working homeless"—"a post-welfare-reform category of strivers fighting to hold onto low-wage jobs the government shepherded them to, jobs that perversely afford them too little money to pay for shelter" (Clines, 2002). A Salvation Army family shelter on the outskirts of St. Louis reports that four fifths of its requests for shelter come from families headed by a wage earner, often a mother willing to commute long hours from the shelter to a fast-food service job. However, if the job pays the minimum wage, she will earn less than half of what she would need to afford a two-bedroom apartment in St. Louis at the going rate (Clines, 2002). As Ehrenreich (2001) says, "You don't need a degree in economics to see that wages are too low and rents too high" (p. 199). Although wages at the top end of the income scale have risen sharply in recent years, wages at the bottom have moved in the opposite direction. In the first quarter of 2000, the poorest 10% of workers earned only 91% of what they earned in 1973, taking inflation into account (Ehrenreich, 2001, p. 203).

Rejecting the official poverty threshold as a meaningful standard, Economic Policy Institute researchers (Boushey, Brocht, Gundersen, & Bernstein, 2001) estimated the cost of living in hundreds of communities across the nation, used those estimates to develop basic family budgets, then counted the number of working families with incomes below the budgets. The national median budget—which includes funds for housing, child care, health care, food, transportation, and taxes—is $33,511 a year for a two-child, two-parent family, roughly twice the poverty threshold for a family that size. Over the period examined, 1997 to 1999, almost 30% of families with one to three children under 12 had incomes below the basic family budget levels. Half of these families included an adult who worked full time.

That means half the families did not include someone with a job. The unemployment rate rose to 6.4% in June 2003, its highest level in 9 years in the worst jobs slump since the early 1980s. This average rate included much higher levels of joblessness for some groups: 19.3% for teenagers, 11.8% for African-Americans, and 8.4% for Hispanics. Consider also what these statistics do not include: "discouraged workers" who are not employed but have stopped actively looking for work, part-time workers seeking but unable to find full-time jobs, and the approximately 2 million people in prison.

Job prospects during the recession of 2001–2002 and the "jobless recovery" that followed were particularly bleak for young adults who were not in school, especially those without a 4-year college degree. Researchers at Northeastern University (Sum, Khatiwada, Pond, & Trub'skyy, 2002) found that 5.2 million 16-to 24-year-olds, almost 15% of all young people in this age group, were neither in school nor had jobs during 2001 and that joblessness among this group surged 12% between 2000 and 2002. In low-income families in central cities, 70% to 80% of the young people who had dropped out of school were jobless. "When you have 5 ½ million young people wandering around without diplomas, without jobs and without prospects, you might as well hand them T-shirts to wear that say 'We're Trouble,' " said Sum, lead author of the study (quoted in Herbert, 2003a). After talking with young people in Chicago without jobs or high school diplomas, Herbert (2003a) offered his own report:

> I did not hear much of anything in the way of aspirations. Whether boys or girls, men or women, those who were interviewed seemed for the most part already defeated. They did not talk about finding the perfect job. They did not talk about being in love and eventually marrying and raising a family. They did not express a desire to someday own their own home. There was, to tell the truth, a remarkable absence of positive comments and emotions of any kind. There was a widespread sense of frustration, and some anger. But mostly there was just sadness.

ECONOMIC POLARIZATION

Wealth, like poverty, is a function of political economy—the politics of who gets what. The gap between rich and poor in the United States more than doubled between 1979 and 2000, according to an analysis of government data by the Center for Budget and Policy Priorities (Browning, 2003). The analysis shows the richest 1% in 2000 had more money to spend after taxes than the bottom 40%. Economic disparity between rich and poor was greater in 2000 than in any year since 1979 when the government began collecting this data.

A smaller breakdown of the income spectrum offers a clearer picture of the trend. An analysis of the after-tax incomes of the top 1% of households between 1979 and 1997 showed most of the gains this group enjoyed actually went to the top 0.1% of individuals with incomes of more than $790,000, and almost half of those gains went to 13,000 taxpayers with incomes of at least $3.6 million and an average income of $17 million (Piketty & Saez, 2001; cited in Krugman, 2002). Between 1992 and 2000, the 400 wealthiest taxpayers more than doubled their share of all income in the U.S., while their tax burden dropped sharply, from 26.4% to 22.3%. Had the tax cuts passed in 2003 been in effect, these 400 taxpayers would have averaged a tax rate of only 17.5% (Johnston, 2003).

Geographically as well as economically, rich and poor live apart. Across the nation, concentration of wealth in affluent (and largely White) suburbs has gone hand-in-hand with concentration of poverty in cities (largely populated by people of color). A pattern seen starkly in New Jersey and Connecticut, the nation's most prosperous states, can be found in many others as well: "enormously wealthy suburbs and almost universally distressed cities" (Herszenhorn, 2001, p. 39). In communities like Stamford, Connecticut, people seeking low-wage jobs, such as cleaning office buildings, cannot afford to live in the area.

Almost all the nation's metropolitan regions now have central areas of concentrated poverty. Ghettoization increased sharply in cities in the Northeast in the 1970s and in the Midwest in the 1980s. Orfield (1997) explains the process:

> Throughout the United States, people move "up and out," taking their economic and social resources with them .... Pushed by concentrated need, pulled by concentrated resources, polarization gathers force. In blighted central city neighborhoods and decaying inner suburbs, poverty and social needs concentrate, racial segregation increases, and poor people grow more isolated from the functional economy and the middle class. (p. 2)

Between 1970 and 1990, the number of people living in high-poverty census tracts (with poverty rates of at least 40%) almost doubled, although the total number of poor people increased by only 37%. In 1990, one third of all poor African-Americans lived in these high-poverty areas, compared with only 6% of all poor Whites (Jargowsky, 1997). From 1980 to 1990, counties containing the nation's 25 largest cities accounted for almost all the increase nationwide in the number of poor school-age children (U.S. General Accounting Office, 1997).

This did not just happen. Government policies beginning in the 1930s encouraged racial and economic segregation. Consider, as just one example, the work of the Home Owners' Loan Corporation, created during the early years of the New Deal as part of a federal initiative to lower the value of urban housing in order to create a market for single-family homes built outside the city:

> The Home Owners' Loan Corporation ... went into Brooklyn and mapped the population of all 66 neighborhoods in the borough, block by block, finding and noting on their maps the location of the residence of every black, Latino, Jewish, Italian, Irish, and Polish family they could find. Then they assigned ratings to each neighborhood based on its ethnic makeup. They distributed the demographic maps to banks and held the banks to a certain standard when loaning money for homes and rental. If the ratings went down, the value of housing property went down. ("Ghettoization," 2001)

The corporation finished its work in the 1940s. Whereas African-Americans in Brooklyn had been the least physically segregated group in the borough in the 1930s, by 1950 they were the most segregated. All were concentrated in the Bedford-Stuyvesant neighborhood, which became the largest Black ghetto in the United States.

The GI bill of 1944 and the government mortgage guarantees, federal mortgage interest deductions, and Interstate Highway Act of 1956 that followed used public money and tax incentives to enable millions of families, largely White, to move "up and out" of cities. "Eight million free college educations and 16 million new suburban homesteads later, these measures had utterly transformed the U.S. landscape. The suburbanization of production and consumption followed soon after. Supermarkets and shopping malls sprang up across the nation" (Ruben, 2001, p. 439). By the 1970s, most job opportunities were in the suburbs; by the 1980s, this included manufacturing jobs, most of which were in suburban industrial parks. Cities paid the price, of course. As many people who could move out did, tax bases declined. As a succession of federal administrations supported the process, cash-strapped cities became home to largely non-White populations.

After her year-long experimental effort to make ends meet on wages from bottom-level jobs, Ehrenreich (2001) was surprised by the disbelief she encountered back in her upper-middle-class life—"You were *where*, doing *what*?" (p. 216)—as if the world of poverty did not exist at all. She speculates that the inability of the nonpoor to "see" the poor arises in part because their paths so rarely cross.

> As public schools and other public services deteriorate, those who can afford to do so send their children to private schools and spend their off-hours in private spaces—health clubs, for example, instead of the lo-

cal park. They don't ride on public buses and subways. They withdraw from mixed neighborhoods into distant suburbs, gated communities, or guarded apartment towers; they shop in stores that, in line with the prevailing "market segmentation," are designed to appeal to the affluent alone. Even the affluent young are increasingly unlikely to spend their summer learning how the "other half" lives, as lifeguards, waitresses, or housekeepers at resort hotels. *The New York Times* reports that they now prefer career-relevant activities like summer school or interning in an appropriate professional setting. (Ehrenreich, 2001, p. 217)

BUDGETS AND TAXES

Although the rich can withdraw from public spaces and services if they wish, the poor cannot. Welfare "reform" and a postrecession jobless recovery are unfolding in the context of the worst budget crises for states since World War II. Facing massive shortfalls, states across the nation cut social programs and funding for public schools in 2002 and 2003. While the Bush Administration was proposing cuts that would eliminate federally funded child care for 200,000 children over the next 5 years and after-school programs for 570,000 children in 2004 alone, states cut child care assistance for low-income working families as well as funding for prekindergarten and after-school programs (Children's Defense Fund, 2003). Twenty-three states reduced child-care subsidies for poor families between 2001 and 2003 (U.S. General Accounting Office, 2003a).

"School finances across the country are teetering on horrendous," said analyst Michael Griffith of the Education Commission of the States, a Denver-based research group (quoted in Dillon, 2003e). At the end of the 2002–2003 school year, Oklahoma City closed seven schools. In Alabama, 38 of the state's 129 school districts were on the brink of bankruptcy. Birmingham closed nine schools before the 2003–2004 year began. Boston closed five schools and eliminated 400 teaching jobs along with 600 other positions. Teachers in Toledo, Ohio, Norwich, Connecticut, and Vista, California, also lost their jobs (Dillon, 2003e).

In the spring of 2002, district officials in Tulsa, Oklahoma, offered 11 training sessions for volunteers willing to fill in for teachers after the district announced it could no longer afford to pay substitutes. In Tucson, Arizona, principals asked parents to bring in toilet paper and sponges to barter for other school supplies (Romano, 2002). In Albert Lea, Minnesota, schools stopped providing bus transportation within a 2-mile radius of schools unless families were willing and able to pay a monthly fee of $30 per student. "[It's] pretty severe," said Superintendent David

Prescott. "Minnesota winters get pretty cold, and to have a first-grader walking to school is not a good idea" (quoted in Ahmad, 2002).

More than 100 mostly rural school districts in Oregon, Wyoming, Colorado, New Mexico, South Dakota, Arkansas, and Louisiana shortened the school week to 4 days, Monday through Thursday, to cut costs for the 2001–2002 year (Reid, 2002). In Oregon, 84 of the state's 198 districts lopped days off the end of the 2002–2003 year (Dillon, 2003b). "During the Great Depression we didn't close schools. We didn't close schools during World War II. Are we the most civically irresponsible generation in Oregon in 100 years?" wondered a physics teacher at Hillsboro High School, where the school year ended 17 days early (quoted in Herbert, 2003b).

The state budget crises unfolded in the context of the mammoth federal tax cut of 2003—"tax relief" the Bush Administration claimed would benefit "everyone who pays taxes," but that turned out not to. At the last minute, Congressional negotiators deleted provisions in the bill that would have allowed 6.5 million minimum-wage families to receive an increase in the child tax credit along with others. The midnight-hour change affected almost 12 million children in low-income families, one in every six under 17. Including these families would have cost approximately $3.5 million, a drop in the bucket in the total cost of the bill, estimated by the Administration to be $350 billion and by critics to be closer to $1 trillion over a 10-year period. In July 2003, the Pentagon doubled an earlier estimate of occupation costs in Iraq to almost $4 billion a month for at least the first 9 months of 2003 (Firestone & Shanker, 2003). In September 2003, the Congressional Budget Office predicted a cumulative budget deficit of at least $2.3 trillion by 2011 (Firestone, 2003).

All this mediates against any expansion of scaled-back social programs and jeopardizes maintenance of programs even at present levels. In 2003, the Administration proposed billions of dollars in cuts for food stamp and child nutrition programs and for health care for the poor along with tighter eligibility requirements for a range of programs benefiting the poor, such as the earned income tax credit and subsidized school lunches (Pear, 2003a), despite warnings that this would lead to an increase in the number of hungry, undernourished children and in the number of *eligible* children deterred from the program (Freedberg, 2003). Welfare "reform" that makes many poor children poorer, a largest-ever federal deficit on top of a huge tax cut wildly skewed toward the wealthy, states dangerously strapped for cash, a recovery after months of recession with few jobs, social segregation along economic as well as racial lines—none of this pushes us toward either more equality or less poverty. This is not to say, however, that no one benefits from this state of affairs. Poor mothers and children largely do not, but many others do.

ANOTHER PERSPECTIVE ON "DEPENDENCY"

Designed to "cure" poor mothers of their "dependence" on "handouts," the welfare overhaul of 1996 pushed them in massive numbers into low-wage jobs on which others depend and often profit. The political question of who gets what is intimately bound up with beliefs about who *should* get what. Who should have plenty to eat and the finest food, who merely enough to survive, and who perhaps not even that? Who should have a comfortable home, who little more than a roof over his or her head, and who nothing more than the streets? Which children should be allowed to attend ("assigned to") one of the nation's best schools, which to schools with competent teachers and minimal standards of safety and sanitation, and which to schools that are chronically short staffed, with too few books, in crumbling buildings? Who gets a say in how these questions are answered and institutionalized in social policies and practices? What political clout do the poor have, given the astonishing concentration of wealth in the society in the last few decades?

The poor today, as they have for decades, often evoke either anger or pity, but rarely outrage and advocacy in the face of the deep injustice and exploitation that fester in a system that generates inequalities on the scale we are now witnessing. Writing about his work with illiterate peasants in Brazil in the mid-1900s, Freire (1970/1990) challenged popular perceptions of his students "as the pathology of the healthy society … marginals need[ing] to be 'integrated,' 'incorporated' into the healthy society that they have 'forsaken'" (pp. 60–61). In actuality, Freire (1970/1990) argued, "the oppressed are not 'marginals' … living 'outside' society. They have always been 'inside'—inside the structure which made them 'beings for others'" (p. 61). The poor in this country similarly are not "marginal," but rather are central players in the society, crucial to its workings, albeit often as "beings for others."

Consider the role of the working poor in a market economy. Unable to support their own families, they provide a wealth of services to others (Chamberlin, 1999). They care for other people's children, aging family members, and suburban lawns. They clean private homes and public restrooms. They assist teachers, nurses, dentists, and veterinarians. They wait tables and stock grocery shelves and vending machines. They move from place to place to pick onions, tomatoes, grapes, and apples on farms owned by others. Because they earn a pittance for this back-breaking labor, others reap the benefits of cheap produce. Reflecting on her year in the world of the working poor, Ehrenreich (2001) describes the social relationships involved: gifts given and received.

> When someone works for less pay than she can live on—when, for example, she goes hungry so that you can eat more cheaply and conveniently—then she has made a great sacrifice for you, she has made you a gift of some part of her abilities, her health, and her life. The "working poor," as they are approvingly termed, are in fact the major philanthropists of our society. They neglect their own children so that the children of others will be cared for; they live in substandard housing so that other homes will be shiny and perfect; they endure privation so that inflation will be low and stock prices high. To be a member of the working poor is to be an anonymous donor, a nameless benefactor, to everyone else. (p. 221)

Because another job is not always easy to find or necessarily any better, workers in bottom-level jobs endure a host of indignities: bosses who treat them like children, rules and regulations that presume they cannot be trusted, "superiors" who push them around because they can. The class-action and individual lawsuits employees in 28 states have filed against Wal-Mart bring to light something more than indignities: exploitation of low-wage workers that easily comes to be seen as "just the way things are" or as a price that just has to be paid. In the first of 40 such lawsuits to go to trial, a federal jury in Portland, Oregon, in 2002 found Wal-Mart guilty of forcing employees to work overtime without pay. Dozens of employees testified that managers pressured them to clock out after 40 hours but keep working—a practice, lawyers say, that enables the company to "squeez[e] tens of millions of dollars of free work out of its employees each year" (Greenhouse, 2002). "Because it's such a small community, jobs aren't that good here," testified a former lawn and garden manager for Wal-Mart in Pendleton, Oregon. "You held on to your job .... I feared getting fired" (quoted in Greenhouse, 2002).

An investigative series published in *The New York Times* and a documentary shown on PBS on the shocking disregard for workers' safety at McWane, Inc.,[1] underscores a more horrifying level of exploitation of the working poor. At Tyler Pipe, a cast-iron pipe foundry in East Texas owned by McWane, three workers have died and hundreds have been hurt since 1995. In 2002, Guadalupe Garcia Jr. was crushed by a truck but survived after doctors amputated both his legs. Mr. Garcia and the truck driver both blamed safety hazards for the accident: poor lighting, inadequate training, and shoddy maintenance on the truck. Mr. Garcia, who spoke out only after the newspaper series was published, said supervisors repeatedly ordered him to take dangerous shortcuts to keep production moving (Barstow & Bergman, 2003a). McWane subsequently was fined $196,000 for new safety violations—a fine many regarded as far too light. "These are things [the safety violations] that kill people," said Margaret Seminario, director of safety and health at the A.F.L.-C.I.O. "Here you have very, very serious hazards, an employer with an atrocious record. And you get basically a slap on the wrist" (quoted in Barstow & Bergman, 2003b). A 9-month investigation by *The Times*, PBS, and the Canadian Broadcasting Corporation found that McWane, which operates plants in 10 states and Canada, has recorded more than 4,600 injuries, racked up more than 400 safety violations (four times as many as its major competitors combined), and has violated pollution laws and emission limits more than 450 times since 1995.

Unpaid work, mangled bodies, loss of life—these things are visible, measurable, and documentable if someone takes up the project. Social stratification and inequality exact "hidden injuries" as well (Sennett & Cobb, 1993). Socially induced shame is taught and learned. A broad public discourse propagates an invidious notion of moral superiority and inferiority. Whereas the well-to-do are often construed as "risk takers," duly rewarded for their hard work and entrepreneurial spirit, the poor are pitted against each other through a race-coded discourse that casts "whites who suffer the effects of declining wages, benefits, and job security" as "deserving," and "blacks who a priori are stigmatized as potential welfare recipients" as "undeserving" (Matsuda, 1997; cited in Munger, 2001, p. 7)—that is, as people who must be forced to work,

[1] A joint investigation by the PBS program "Frontline," *The New York Times*, and the Canadian Broadcasting Corporation led to a documentary, "A Dangerous Business," broadcast on PBS on January 9, 2003, and to a series of reports published in the *Times* January 8–10, 2003. Neil Docherty and David Rummel produced the documentary. David Barstow, Lowell Bergman, James Sandler, and Robin Stein wrote the articles for the *Times*.

with more stick than carrot, no matter how poor the pay, how grueling the work, or how detrimental the consequences for children.

Of course, this is often a no-win situation. Many people who play by the rules and do as the larger society demands still do not earn enough to live free of economic distress and socially induced shame. They learn and their children learn, because they are taught—through books, billboards, movies, the rhetoric of policy making, the messages inherent in the quality of schooling they are offered, and so on—to feel ashamed.

Consider the lesson internalized by this mother and daughter in an incident Hancock (2002) recalls from a bus ride in the Bronx:

> A boisterous threesome of junior high girls bounded to the seat opposite me, giggling and hollering. As we pulled up to a red light, their happy chatter stopped so abruptly that I looked up from my newspaper. Two friends were prodding the third. "What's up? What's wrong?" they asked their friend. The wiry girl drooped in her seat, her school uniform vest bunched up to her neck, as she looked out the bus window. Outside, a group of five older women dressed in orange work vests were picking up litter around a city garbage can next to the traffic light. "It's Mama," the youngster said. "She told me she was working in an office." Apparently, the mother was too ashamed to tell her daughter she was a WEP [Work Experience Program] worker for the city, picking up trash in the Bronx. (p. 279)

Consider, finally, 12-year-old Nahem's cry of protest in an essay he wrote while homeless and living in a hotel. Nahem wrote the essay for a class at Manhattan's P.S. 151 and it subsequently was published in *The New York Times*:

> As I lay in bed crying myself to sleep ... I could not bring myself to overcome the fear of what was happening to me. Over and over again I keep telling myself that I don't deserve this. I'm only 12 years old. I feel so alone. People in school call me a hotel kid. I don't think it's because they don't like me. I just think that they are afraid that if I am the same as them and I am homeless then something could happen beyond their control leaving them homeless just like me. It seems like people are so afraid of ending up where I'm at that they want to punish me for reminding them that being homeless is possible. They have no right to punish me for something I have no control over. I'm just a little boy, living in a hotel, petrified, wanting to know what's going to happen to me.
>
> People should stop trying to make children who are homeless feel ashamed. I don't steal, rob people, use drugs, stay out all night, or play hookey from school. If being a poor child living in a rich city is a crime then I'm guilty. I am not a hotel kid. I am a child who lives in a hotel. I am

> just like most other little boys. I like to play baseball, ride bikes, and go to the movies with my friends. It's strange, but I really like when the lights go off in the movies because then I'm no longer a homeless child. I'm just a person watching the movie like everyone else. ("As welfare hotels," 1990)

Nahem's insight that the poor differ from others only to the extent that they lack the money needed to live in accord with social norms, if taken to heart, brings us face-to-face with the social injustice of poverty in this wealthiest nation on earth. The suffering that comes with the territory of poverty is not deserved. Poor people do not choose to be poor. They do not cause poverty. Poverty results rather from an ill-distribution of social goods—primarily power, wealth, and opportunity—and is fed by apathy and exploitation. Harmful to the poor, poverty can be quite profitable for others. Low-wage workers keep business operating costs down. Public schools run by for-profit companies, prisons run as private businesses, and private foster-care operations all funnel public money into private hands through the provision of "services" to a population that is almost entirely poor. The growing debt industry, now a "$5 billion-a-year trade in financial services for the bankless," is draining central cities of what little wealth is there (Williams, 2001, p. 84). Check-cashing outlets in 1993 cashed 150 million checks for people without access to a bank or unable to meet minimum balance requirements, and charged $700 million in fees. Rent-to-own stores that often end up charging five times as much as people would pay for furniture or appliances in retail stores are now a $3.7 billion-a-year business.

Tolerance of poverty that is neither natural nor necessary flies in the face of the long-standing ideals that give this society its heart and soul: faith in the promise of each and every child, belief in the value of providing equal educational opportunity, and an impulse to be compassionate and to recognize our shared vulnerability before the unpredictable twists and turns of life that leave all of us, eventually, in need of other people's help. And these are not merely ideals. Our society funds and supports, however inadequately and unevenly, a system of public schooling dedicated, at least rhetorically, to the intellectual growth and development of all children. We fund and support, however begrudgingly, social programs designed to help at least some people: the elderly through Social Security, the disabled through SSI (Supplemental Security Income), the hungry through the provision of food stamps, and poor children through Head Start. At the same time, a morally laden discourse of deserving with a long history has both reflected and shaped a public sensibility that mediates against outrage and advocacy. Society tolerates concentrations of wealth and poverty that not only put millions of children at grave risk, but jeopardize its own democratic foundations. Although the alleged shortcomings of welfare mobilized public sentiment against a federal guarantee of help, the child poverty that has endured long past this "reform" has not.

The next chapter considers the social experience of poverty and some of the injustices poor children suffer.

4

Living in Poverty

> *When you ride on the Number 6 train [in New York City] from East 59th Street to the racial cutoff point at 96th, you pass beneath an area in which 2,400 private doctors, most of them highly qualified, have their offices and in which the ratio of doctors to residents is approximately 60 to 1,000. When you leave the subway at Brook Avenue, you are in a neighborhood in which the ratio is two per 1,000.*
>
> —*Kozol (1995, pp. 172–173)*

> *It is common, among the nonpoor, to think of poverty as a sustainable condition—austere, perhaps, but they get by somehow, don't they? They are "always with us." What is harder for the nonpoor to see is poverty as acute distress: The lunch that consists of Doritos or hot dog rolls, leading to faintness before the end of the shift. The "home" that is also a car or a van. The illness or injury that must be "worked through," with gritted teeth, because there's no sick pay or health insurance and the loss of one day's pay will mean no groceries for the next.*
>
> —*Ehrenreich (2001, p. 214)*

Ten-year-old Brittany Lyles lives with her mother, sister, niece, and brother in a public housing complex in Belzoni, Mississippi, the catfish capital of the nation. Brittany's mother earns $6.20 an hour cutting heads off catfish—one a second, 600 an hour, 28,800 a day—at Delta Pride Catfish in the Mississippi Delta. The job, which she has had for 10 years, is grueling, cold (the room is kept at about 60°), and dangerous. Ms. Lyles has cut her hand badly three times and lost the tip of one thumb to a saw. She keeps the job, she says, because she needs the pay:

> Their goal is to get as many fish processed as possible. Mine is to leave the plant every day with all my body parts .... I hate the job ... but it's the best job there is around here, because the other factories are piecework. I

> have to have a job where I know what I'm going to take home at the end of the day. (quoted in Shirk, Bennett, & Aber, 1999, p. 208)

Ms. Lyles works overtime as often as she can, but the work is seasonal and her wages generally bring the family of five up to just over half the federal poverty line. Ms. Lyles is now about $12,000 in debt. She shares a car with a friend, another single mother, and the family has no phone. Still, these are relatively good times—better than when the whole family lived in a run-down, two-bedroom trailer, better than when two of the children shared a single room in a boardinghouse with their mother, and better than when Ms. Lyles worked in a chicken processing factory an hour and a half away. Then she was away from home everyday from 1 o'clock in the afternoon until 2:30 in the morning.

Until 11-year-old Jamall Roper, his three younger siblings, and their 55-year-old grandmother and guardian, Arlene Cruz, moved into a short-term shelter apartment in New York City, the family was homeless for almost 2 months. Jamall's grandmother gathered Jamall and his brothers and sisters from foster homes in New Jersey 4 years ago, and the family survived on what she earned working two low-wage jobs, one in a supermarket and the other as a hospital aide, plus food stamps. When her health failed and the car broke down, the family's nightmare of homelessness began. During that time, Ms. Cruz struggled to deliver the four children to their public school in East Harlem, starting each day from a different shelter for the homeless and returning each night to the Emergency Assistance Unit in the South Bronx, the sole portal to New York City's shelter system. There, along with some of the other 5,500 people seeking shelter, they would wait for a late-night bus to take them somewhere, anywhere, to sleep. Sometimes that happened, sometimes not, in which case the family slept on benches or the floor. "It's almost like getting punished for hitting bottom—something you couldn't help," Ms. Cruz said. "You see homeless people and you feel bad and then you turn around and realize, 'I'm homeless. I am homeless with all these children.'" (quoted in Bernstein, 2001a)

Seven-year-old Jessica lived for a year in an illegal 12-by-15-foot room for which her parents paid $300 a month, down a tunnel-like hallway in a building with more than 300 pending housing code violations. Jessica shared the windowless room and its one bed with her mother, father, and two brothers. The children and their mother left their dirt-poor life in a Mexican village 7 years ago to join the father in the United

States. Here, Jessica's parents earned $250 together in a good week as street-corner flower vendors in New York City.

> Jessica is in many ways the saddest of the three [children] .... She has outgrown her innocence of poverty, knowing now that most families, even poor ones, do not sleep piled on one bed, shrinking from a father's oversized anger, drifting from one basement to the next. She has grown uncomfortable around strangers, and unsheathes her vivid smile only when she is sure they are not watching: their eyes have become her eyes, their prejudice has become her shame. (Alvarez, 1996, p. A1)

Jessica's nightmare did not end so much as change when the family was evicted from the tiny room after her father was deported.

The Martinez family for years has migrated between Texas's Rio Grande Valley and southeastern Michigan. The family of 10 (mother, father, and eight boys) earns about $15,000 a year picking asparagus, strawberries, cherries, blueberries, grapes, and apples. Jose, the oldest child, who is now in college, started picking berries when he was in the second grade: "We needed the money and me and all my brothers were an essential part of the family's economy," Jose said (quoted in Rothenberg, 1998, pp. 272–273). That has not changed. "Even as we speak," he said, "my little brothers are out there picking blueberries" (p. 276).

Nine-year-old Shakeina Merchant lives in a foster home in Freeport, New York, with her younger brother and sister. The children entered the foster care system 3 years ago when their mother was charged with neglect. They stay with their father on weekends; Shakeina wishes she could live with him all the time. "Friday is my best day," she said. "That's the day my daddy comes to get me. We stay here together, and that's what I like. We cook together and do things. Mrs. David [Shakeina's foster mother] is okay, but I'd rather stay here all the time" (Hewlett & West, 1998, p. 116). Shakeina's father was awarded custody of the three children 6 months earlier and was told he could take them out of foster care if he could find a place for them to live—something better than the single room he now rents. On the $250 a week Mr. Merchant earns working on a loading dock, that has not been possible. "They say I can have my kids if I find housing, but there's nothing they can do to help me find housing," he said (quoted in Hewlett & West, 1998, p. 117). "The way I look at it, if they gave me just half the money they're spending on foster care, I can make it .... But the system doesn't work for people who want to take care of their own" (p. 117).

Brittany, Jamall, Jessica, Jose, Shakeina, and their sisters and brothers are among the more than 27 million children living in poverty or "near poverty"—that is, in families with incomes below 200% of the federal poverty line (Lu, 2003). Not surprisingly, many of them are not doing well in school. Jamall, an honors student, has started falling asleep in class and crying through counseling sessions. "I think they don't want us to have our education. Because they don't give us enough sleep [at homeless shelters] to not fall asleep in class," he told a reporter (Bernstein, 2001a, p. A1). Months earlier, Jamall's sister, Tara, had earned a 100 "for her wishful account of a family Thanksgiving and a 90 on a report about 'A Christmas Carol.'" However, "when her penmanship became a sleep-deprived scrawl," her grades began to drop. "If something is not done to help this family," Tara's second-grade teacher warned, "four young lives will be destroyed" (quoted in Bernstein, 2001a, p. A1). Jessica does not attend school at all and, at 7, cannot read in Spanish or English. Jessica's mother has not enrolled her in school because she believes (incorrectly) that she would have to show a birth certificate, which she does not have, and because she fears exposing the family's undocumented status (Alvarez, 1996).

Brittany is in classes for the gifted and always makes the honor roll at her school, and Jose has completed a year of college. He now has a summer job working with a home-study program for children of migrant farmworkers. He visits them in labor camps and in local rental housing every 2 weeks to tutor and encourage them to stay in school. "I want to get ahead," Jose said. "When I finish university and have a good job, it will be time for my parents to stop working. I wish I had enough money right now to say to my mother and father, 'You've worked hard enough. That's it. You don't need to work anymore' " (Rothenberg, 1998, pp. 275–276).

Stories like Britanny's and Jose's are inspiring, even reassuring, but do not alter the social reality: As a group, poor children bear the brunt of almost every imaginable social ill (Children's Defense Fund, 2002c; Duncan & Brooks-Gunn, 1997; National Commission on Children, 1991; Polakow, 1993, 2003; Sherman, 1997). This includes not only hunger and homelessness, but also untreated sickness and chronic conditions, such as asthma (Perez-Pena, 2003), tooth decay (Goldberg, 1999), lead poisoning (Needleman, Riess, Tobin, Biesecker, & Greenhouse, 1996), and other effects of environmental pollution (Books, 2000; Friedrich, 2000; Kozol, 1995). Perhaps most devastating is the sometimes hidden but nevertheless debilitating anxiety created by living in crowded, run-down spaces with chronic shortages of money and fears of eviction, family dissolution, and random street violence (Canada, 1995; Hicks-Bartlett, 2000; Kling, Liebman, & Katz, 2001). Poor children get sick and die more often than others. One national study found that poor children are 50% more likely than other children to die during childhood (Sherman, 1997). In Washington, DC, mortality rates for African-American infants exceed those in 56 nations, including the Bahamas, Barbados, Fiji, and Jamaica (Children's Defense Fund, 2002c).

The pages that follow describe some of the major social problems—problems with social roots—that affect children's lives, including their school lives. Such an overview necessarily only scratches the surface, but perhaps suggests the scope of the social injustice poor children suffer.

ENVIRONMENTAL INJUSTICE

Far more industrial plants, waste facilities, and other potential polluters are located in low-income communities, especially communities of color, than in other places (Children's Defense Fund, 2001b). Children who live in these communities suffer from environmentally induced health problems in alarming numbers. Poor children do not just happen to get sick more than other children and suffer more health problems; they are *made* sick by the places they are forced to live. "Black youths in Harlem, central Detroit, the South Side of Chicago and Watts have about the same probability of dying by age 45 as whites nationwide do by age 65, and most of this premature death is due not to violence, but to illness. A third of poor black 16-year-old girls in urban areas will not reach their 65th birthdays" (Epstein, 2003, p. 12).

Consider, first, lead poisoning, perhaps "the most serious and most common environmental health hazard for children" (Children's Defense Fund, 2001a, pp. 38–39), "a problem that has been ghettoized" (Landrigan, quoted in Friedrich, 2000, p. 3057), and a problem the Centers for Disease Control and Prevention (CDC; 2003a) regards as "entirely preventable." Although children's exposure to lead decreased significantly after the U.S. Environmental Protection Agency (EPA) banned lead in paint and gasoline in the 1970s, 434,000 children 1 to 5 years old still have elevated blood-lead levels (CDC, 2003b). At greatest risk are poor children living in older housing, especially children of color. CDC (2003b) statistics show that more than one in every five African-American children and one in every eight Mexican-American children living in housing built before 1946 have elevated blood-lead levels. Poisoning rates are eight times higher among low-income children than children from upper income families, and five times higher among African-American than White children. In some neighborhoods, one third of all preschoolers are poisoned by lead.[1]

Even at low levels, lead poisoning can cause learning disabilities, hyperactivity, and behavioral disorders, and at higher levels, mental retardation and even death. A 1996 study found that boys (first grade through age 11) with relatively high bone-lead levels had more attention problems, were more aggressive, and were more anxious and depressed than their peers. "If the findings ... extend to the population of U.S. children, the contribution of lead to delinquent behavior would be substantial," the researchers concluded. "Altered social behavior may be among the earliest expressions of lead toxicity" (Needleman et al., 1996, p. 369).

If families seeking a cheap source of protein fish in water contaminated by PCBs, common in areas with old manufacturing plants, children can be exposed to these toxins as well (Friedrich, 2000), and if pesticides are widely used, as they often are to kill cockroaches, poor children face a triple threat. If something is not done, warned Dr. Philip Landrigan of Mount Sinai School of Medicine in New York City, "we're going to perpetuate a population of poor minority kids whose intellects are eroded by toxins like lead, and who will continue for generations to come to be environmentally, medically, and economically disadvantaged in relation to majority kids" (quoted in Friedrich, 2000).

A U.S. General Accounting Office (GAO) study (1999) found that, despite federal regulations requiring lead screening for all children served by Medicaid, this often is not happening. For almost two thirds of the children with elevated lead levels, the screening conducted in conjunction with the GAO study was their first ever. Children enrolled in Medicaid account for 93% of all cases of severe lead poisoning and 60% of all children with elevated blood-lead levels.[2] Yet, even if all children at high risk for lead poisoning were screened, that would not be enough. Screening, even if followed by treatment, addresses symptoms only, not the root problem, which is the lead in the environment. All too often, in a "ludicrous cycle," doctors "find and treat lead-poisoned chil-

---

[1]This information is included in a letter to Sec. Tommy Thompson of the U.S. Department of Health and Human Services, dated April 22, 2002, and signed by 473 organizations and individuals. Retrieved from *http://www.healthlaw.org/pubs/200204.leadsignon.pdf*

[2]Ibid.

dren, only to see them return to their contaminated environment" (Dr. Stephen Marcus; quoted in Kannapell, 1998, p. NJ6). Many states, it seems, have tried to avoid being put in this position by not screening at all (Connolly, 2002, p. A25). As of 2003, no lawsuits against the lead industry had yet gone to trial or been settled.[3]

Asthma, another environmentally related condition that afflicts poor children disproportionately, is growing faster than any other chronic disease in the United States. Between 1980 and 1994, the number of children under 4 years old with asthma mushroomed by 160%. "At the current rate of growth ... the number of asthma cases in 2020 will exceed the projected population of New York and New Jersey combined," the Pew Environmental Health Commission (2000) warned (p. 5). At present, the United States has no national tracking system for asthma; neither are most states equipped to monitor its incidence (Pew Environmental Health Commission, 2000).

Asthma rates are increasing fastest among children of color in low-income communities where pollution, indoors and out, is widespread (Children's Defense Fund, 2001a). In homes with intermittent heat, people sometimes use gas ovens for warmth, but pollutants from stove exhaust can build up and make asthma attacks more likely. Severe triggers, more prevalent in poor urban neighborhoods, include dust mites, cigarette smoke, mold, diesel exhaust, animal hair, rats, and cockroaches. Researcher David Rosenstreich attributes about 25% of all asthma cases in inner cities to roaches (Leary, 1997, p. A18).

A project that included testing every child in a 24-block area of central Harlem for asthma, 2,000 children in all, found one of the highest rates ever documented in the United States: one in every four school-age children. In light of this finding, researchers now believe asthma rates could be much higher than suspected in many other urban neighborhoods as well (Perez-Pena, 2003). "As garbage piles up, so do complaints," *The New York Times* reported after a landfill on Staten Island was closed and, as a consequence, twice as much garbage was routed to a transfer station in the Hunts Point area of the South Bronx (Stewart, 2001). Residents blame garbage truck exhaust and polluted air around

---

[3]Cities, counties, and states have filed suit against lead-pigment manufacturers, however. Rhode Island; 10 counties in California, New Jersey, and Texas; more than 20 cities, including San Francisco, Oakland, Milwaukee, St. Louis, and Newark; seven school districts in California, Texas and Mississippi; and the New York City Housing Authority all have filed or joined suits against lead-pigment manufacturers to force them to clean up hazards or to recover public health costs of lead poisoning (Alliance to End Childhood Lead Poisoning, 2003).

the station for the extraordinarily high rate of asthma in the community. "I can't remember ever being in another place in the United States in which so many children spoke of having difficulty breathing," Kozol (1995) said about the time he spent in the Mott Haven area of the South Bronx (p. 170). Asthma hospitalization rates as much as 21 times higher than in more affluent areas have been found in poor minority neighborhoods in New York City (Center for Children's Health and the Environment, 1999). Almost half of all homeless children in the city are asthmatic (Children's Defense Fund, 2001b).

Even in public schools, poor children face disproportionate environmental risks. "School districts pressed to save money are often enticed by donations of unknowingly contaminated property, seek out the cheapest land, or hire uncertified or poor-quality contractors for environmental assessment" (Center for Health, Environment, and Justice, 2001, p. 3). In densely populated urban districts with little vacant land, new schools often are built on sites where homes and businesses have been condemned or on former industrial property tracts. These communities "face an unfair decision: accept siting on inexpensive contaminated land ... or build on expensive environmentally safer property, depleting funds for teaching resources" (Center for Health, Environment, and Justice, 2001, pp. 19-20).

Sometimes even this bad "choice" is unavailable. In Watsonville, California, the Pajaro Valley Unified School District wants to build a school largely for low-income students of color less than 3,000 feet from the runway of an airport (a violation of airport land-use regulations) and 3,600 feet from a solid waste landfill, which also collects toxic and hazardous wastes. The proposed site, isolated in an industrial zone far from most of the students' homes, is bordered by a cattle feedlot on one side and a freeway on the other. Although other sites are available, "Citizens, farmers and city officials ... from the alternative sites oppose the high school being placed in their area because the students of color would be bused into their neighborhood" (Center for Health, Environment, and Justice, 2001, p. 23).

HEALTH CARE

Far more likely than others to be exposed to environmental toxins, poor children, especially immigrant children, are far less likely to have health insurance and therefore regular medical care. In 2000, 35% of all uninsured children were Latino, even though Latinos comprise only 16.5% of all children in the United States (Holahan, Dubay, & Kenney, 2003). Many factors contribute to this situation. A disproportionate share of immigrant parents work in low-wage jobs that do not offer health benefits. Also, provisions of the 1996 welfare law made many immigrant children ineligible for Medicaid and State Children's Health Insurance Programs (SCHIP) and led families of other children to believe, often incorrectly, that they are ineligible or will be reported to the Immigration and Naturalization Service (INS) if they apply.

> In the mid-1990s, immigration and consular officials began to scrutinize immigrants' use of health care benefits. Immigrants learned that their use of health benefits categorized them as "public charges" (an immigration term for people who depend on public aid), jeopardizing their residency. People deemed public charges can be denied entry to the United States, denied reentry after travel abroad, or refused lawful permanent residency. Some officials told immigrants that to remain in or reenter the United States, they would have to repay Medicaid benefits that they or their children had legitimately received. (Lessard & Ku, 2003, p. 106)

The INS subsequently clarified that use of health care programs such as Medicaid and SCHIP should not be considered in "public charge" determinations. However, many low-income immigrants continue to fear negative repercussions if anyone in the family receives public benefits (Lessard & Ku, 2003).

By the spring of 2003, the economy was floundering badly, the federal deficit was swelling, health care costs were on the rise, states across the nation faced massive budget shortfalls, and Congress passed a large and highly regressive tax cut that promised to further deplete state and federal coffers. The Texas House of Representatives passed a bill that would restrict eligibility for the state-run Medicaid and child health insurance programs, with the likely consequence of 240,000 children and 17,000 pregnant women losing coverage. Tennessee removed 208,000 people, including 55,000 children, from its expanded Medicaid program over a 6-month period. Connecticut legislators passed a law eliminating Medicaid benefits for 23,000 adults and 7,000 children, and Indiana expected 36,000 children to lose coverage under new rules requiring people to reestablish eligibility every few months (Toner & Pear, 2003).

Even before these cutbacks, "a striking rich–poor inequality" shaped children's access to dentists as well as doctors (Goldberg,

1999). The National Institute of Dental Research estimates that 80% of all cavities are concentrated among 25% of all children, most of whom are poor (Goldberg, 1999). The U.S. Surgeon General in 2000 warned of a "silent epidemic" and condemned "profound and consequential disparities in the oral health of our citizens" (U.S. Department of Health and Human Services, 2000). Poor children are twice as likely as others to suffer from tooth decay, often untreated, and about 25% do not see a dentist before they start kindergarten. This, of course, makes learning or even sitting in a classroom difficult. Children with toothaches cannot concentrate. When their teeth literally are rotting, they often just cry (Hurst, 2003).

Low reimbursements for Medicaid patients, a shrinking number of dentists in many communities, and lack of oral health education all contribute to the problem. So, too, does a general prejudice against the poor, suggests Dr. William Kassler, medical director in New Hampshire: "Dentists have made comments like, 'Nothing empties my waiting room faster than one of those patients,' and, 'It's their fault. They're not compliant. They don't pay attention to hygiene. Why don't they take a bath before coming in?'" (quoted in Goldberg, 1999).

CHILD LABOR

Poor children often work to help struggling families make ends meet. Federal child labor law permits children working in agriculture to work at a younger age and do more hazardous tasks than young workers in other environments. Consequently, children in migrant farmworking families who work along with their parents, as many do, are at special risk not only from pesticides sprayed in fields, but also from exhaustion and dehydration from working long hours in the sun, often with dangerous equipment. "They're breathing pesticides, they're often not paid the minimum wage and they often end up dropping out of schools," said Diane Mull, executive director of the Association of Farm Worker Opportunity Programs (Greenhouse, 2000, p. A12). U.S. Department of Labor statistics show the consequences of this double standard for young workers: Although only 6% to 7% of the jobs young people hold are in agriculture, 40% of all work-related deaths among young people are in agriculture (Greenhouse, 2000).

Although their labor generally is unpaid, poor girls are often called on to help their families. In her research on the experience of growing up female and poor in the United States, Dodson (1999) listened to dozens of girls and women talk about "girl's work ... a catchall category of baby-sitting, housecleaning, errand running, attending to people, and sometimes meeting complex family problems" (p. 14). Annette's experience is typical; in her own words:

> My mother came home from the hospital with my baby brother and she was very sick. I never felt the obligation of having to take care of the baby or [my older] brothers. But with all the other work combined ... I would miss days of school in the fourth grade to do the housework. By the time I was thirteen, I would rather stay home and help my mother than go to school. She needed me. (p. 17)

Annette never developed confidence in her schoolwork or became part of a peer group. "She grew into adolescence without a real presence anywhere but at home .... She left school on her sixteenth birthday and was married before her seventeenth. By the time she turned twenty-one, Annette was a divorced unemployed mother of two children" (Dodson, 1999, p. 17).

In families that cannot afford baby-sitters, private child care, cars, washers and dryers, vacations, or meals out, daughters' work often fills the gap. Girls cook, clean, and care for younger brothers, sisters, and cousins; negotiate social-service bureaucracies; attend to stressed parents; and, in some cases, try to protect mothers and siblings from domestic violence. In the process, homework easily becomes a low priority or is forgotten altogether, school attendance falls off, and going to college or even graduating from high school becomes something for which there is simply no time. In their examination of urban youth dropping out of school, Fine and Zane (1991) found that although boys as well as girls in low-income communities drop out more often than others, girls report "family concerns" as the cause far more often than boys. In their study, 37% of the girls cited family issues as the reason they left school compared with only 5% of the boys.

COMMUNITY VIOLENCE

Poor children often grow up in worlds defined by anxiety, uncertainty, or fear. In neighborhoods wracked by random violence, the stress can be unrelenting for families. Jesus Gilberto, a health care provider in the South Bronx, suspects the fear and stress contribute to the prevalence of asthma in many poor communities: "Some of [the asthma problem] is environmental—housing infestation, pesticides, no heat in an apartment. But a great deal is emotional as well. Fear of violence can be a strong constrictive force. If you moved these families into a nice suburb, nine tenths of this feeling of constriction, I'm convinced, would be relieved" (quoted in Kozol, 1995, pp. 173–174). Children who witness shootings, beatings, and other atrocities are at risk of developing post-traumatic stress disorder (PTSD), "the package of symptoms that arises from encountering trauma and being changed by the experience" (Garbarino, 1995, p. 77). In a child, these symptoms include nightmares, aggression, daydreaming, recreating the trauma in play, being easily startled, and losing a basic confidence in life, "his or her belief that life will be long" (Garbarino, 1995, p. 83). PTSD can affect a child's neurochemistry in ways that create significant psychological problems that interfere with learning, behavior in school, and parent–child relationships (Garbarino, 1995).

The United States is the most violent country in the industrialized world (Moore, 2002). Although often random, the violence is not randomly distributed across the country. Poor children, especially poor children of color living in densely populated urban neighborhoods, are victims and witnesses of "community violence" far more often than others. Now regarded as a public health issue, community violence has been linked with the development of PTSD in children as well as adults; with fearfulness, the belief that "harm could come at any time"; and with feelings of betrayal and distrust (National Center for Post-Traumatic Stress Disorder, 2003). Parents and other family members affected by community violence often worry excessively about their children's well-being and blame themselves for being unable to offer protection. They struggle to reassure children while coping with their own fears.

Economists at Princeton University who studied a program that enabled families in high-poverty housing projects in Boston to move to lower poverty areas were surprised by the pervasive, consuming fear of random violence they found and by many mothers' feeling that they needed "to spend every minute of their day making sure their children were safe" (Uchitelle, 2001a, p. BU 4). In her interviews in a large city in the Midwest, Hicks-Bartlett (2000) found mothers worrying constantly about their children's safety and consequently being reluctant to seek employment outside the home. In neighborhoods without libraries, after-school programs, and other extracurricular opportunities common in middle-class neighborhoods, anxious mothers often opt not to seek low-wage work if it means leaving children alone.

FOSTER CARE

Although families themselves can be dangerous places, perhaps no life experience is more traumatic for children than "losing" a mother, father, or other caregiver. Overwhelmingly, children in foster care or at risk of entering it are poor children (Bernstein, 2001b). Ninety-five percent or more of cases labeled "child neglect" might more accurately be described as family poverty (Wexler, 1990, p. 53). "Children were and are taken away from their parents because the family doesn't have a functioning toilet or can't afford to fill a prescription. Children are taken away because the food stamps have run out and the refrigerator is empty. And children are taken away because the family doesn't have a place to live" (Hewlett & West, 1998, p. 16).

With the passage of the Aid to Dependent Children provisions of the Social Security Act of 1935, the number of children in foster care declined dramatically and stayed down for more than two decades. However, out-of-home placements rose again after 1961 when new rules allowed federal dollars to follow poor children into private, nonprofit foster care. When the 1996 welfare law was enacted, for-profit organizations were invited to compete as well for the billions of dollars the federal government spends each year to subsidize the care of children removed from homes judged unfit.[4]

Considerable money is at stake because federal funding for foster care, unlike funding for other child-welfare programs, such as family preservation and support services, is uncapped. "A profit-making feeding frenzy. These corporations are growing almost helter-skelter, without people who know the field or know kids," Paul DeMuro, a former commissioner of children in Pennsylvania, warned at the time (quoted in Bernstein, 1997). Public agencies have their own stake in maintaining a large foster care population as "each case of child abuse or neglect unlocks significant state and federal funds, not only for the child welfare agency directly concerned but for a satellite ring of sub-

[4]Companies that stand to benefit from the change in the foster care regulations include managed-mental-health-care giants like Magellan Health Services and youth-care chains like the 2,500-bed Youth Services International, started a few years ago by the founder of the quick oil-change franchise Jiffy Lube (Bernstein, 1997).

stitute caregivers, therapists, and family court lawyers" (Hewlett & West, 1998, p. 119).

The foster care population has increased dramatically in the last 10 years and now exceeds 500,000 (American Academy of Child and Adolescent Psychiatry, 2002). This number almost certainly will continue to grow as mothers unable to find jobs or child care lose any form of public assistance under the provisions of the 1996 welfare law.[5] In New Jersey, dozens of adolescents in foster care are now locked up in juvenile detention centers—often, child welfare officials admit, because they cannot find anyplace else for them. "Awaiting placement in detentions is one of the dirty little secrets of the system," said Bart Lubow of the Annie E. Casey Foundation, a national child-advocacy organization. "It's an issue across the country" (quoted in Jones & Kaufman, 2003). In the most troubled counties in New Jersey, overcrowding compounds the problem. A facility in Camden County, built to house 37 children, routinely has almost 100. Rooms designed for one child accommodate four (Jones & Kaufman, 2003).

FAMILY HOMELESSNESS

Family homelessness, often the prelude to family dissolution and always a traumatic experience, has risen alarmingly in the 21st century. Families, among the fastest growing segment of this population, now comprise 40% of the homeless (National Coalition of the Homeless, 2002). The need for shelter in New York City became so great in the summer of 2002 that, until ordered to stop by a Manhattan judge, the city administration sent homeless families with children to an old jail in the Bronx (Kaufman, 2002). Advocates for the homeless protested vigorously not only because of the awful message this sends to the families and the broader public, that poor people belong in jail, but also because lead exposure in the facility exceeds EPA limits (Cardwell, 2002).

A growing shortage of affordable housing combined with shrinking wages has contributed to the rise in homelessness among families (National Coalition for the Homeless, 2002). In its annual assessment of the affordability of rental housing, the National Low Income Housing Coalition (2002) found that, for the fourth consecutive year, in no county in the United States does a minimum wage job provide enough income for a

---

[5]The foster care program was growing five times faster and costing the federal government 11 times more per child than AFDC when this program was abolished in 1996 (Bernstein, 1997).

household to afford the area's "fair market rent" for a two-bedroom home without paying more than 30% of the family's income, the accepted standard of affordability. The median wage required to be able to afford a two-bedroom home at the average fair market rent is $14.66 an hour, almost three times the federal minimum wage. In Marin County, California, where the gap between rents and wages is largest, a worker would have to earn $37.30 an hour to afford a two-bedroom home.

Michael's story, shared by Polakow (2003), captures the terror homelessness brings into the lives of children. Born into homelessness after his mother, when 8 months pregnant, fled from one state to another to escape his father's violence, Michael had been homeless four times by the time he was 8 years old.

> During the latest episode of homelessness, when the family fled from drug and gang violence at a public housing site, Michael was so traumatized, that as I drove the family to a shelter, he lay on the floor of my car, screaming and clutching his pillow as he cried: "I hate this life—why can't I live in a place like other kids—it's not fair—I won't have friends no more at school—it's the worst thing in the world when you don't got no home. I never never want to go in that shelter ..." Michael lay crying on the floor, curled up in a fetal position, and refused to leave the car to set foot in the shelter. An hour later, after being coaxed inside he sat on the stairway, angrily shouting about his mother, "Why does she do this to us—why can't we have a regular home like other kids—I can't go to school no more 'cos my friends will find out I'm in a shelter—I hate her, I hate her—I'm gonna run away from here ..."

For 3 months Michael moved between the shelter and a "welfare motel." During this time he had nightmares, became very fearful, and lashed out at classmates. He ran away from school twice in the middle of the day and was suspended. After the family got a more permanent place to live, Michael's father tracked them down and started threatening Michael's mother again. "At that point Michael snapped. One afternoon the school janitor found him trying to crawl into the furnace, saying he wanted to die. Soon after, he was hospitalized for 14 days at a children's psychiatric unit" (Polakow, 1993, p. 95). When Polakow (1993) visited him in the hospital he told her, "I don't got no reason to live" (p. 95).

SOCIALLY CREATED DISTRESS

The plethora of statistics brought together in this chapter offers crude documentation of enormous pain, suffering, distress, and shameful injustice—shameful in the sense that much of it could be eradicated or at least ameliorated. No one chooses to live in substandard housing, in neighborhoods wracked by violence, or in communities polluted by toxins any more than anyone chooses to be unable to find a doctor or dentist to treat a son or daughter. These choices are foisted on the poor in a society that concentrates power and wealth in fewer and fewer hands, with the inevitable consequence that poverty and powerlessness are concentrated as well. In the powerful words of a young woman, Kozol (1995) quotes:

> If you weave enough bad things into the fibers of a person's life—sickness and filth ... a prison here, sewage there, drug dealers here, the homeless people over there, then give us the very worst schools anyone could think of, hospitals that keep you waiting for ten hours, police that don't show up when someone's dying ... you can guess that life will not be very nice and children will not have much sense of being glad of who they are. (pp. 39–40)

Policies and laws are human creations, of course, expressions of ideas or of compromises among competing ideas, aligned with particular social visions. The injustice this chapter documents is in no sense necessary; that it exists nevertheless betrays a society that has agreed to tolerate socially created distress. That the poor suffer because they are poor and therefore powerless has ceased to be a cause of societal shame, if it ever was. The nation prides itself on its military and economic predominance in the world, not on how it treats its most vulnerable members.

In congressional debates leading up to the welfare "reform" of 1996, political leaders referred to mothers receiving public assistance as "wolves" and "alligators," and as people who regard parenthood as a "cheap joke."[6] Such disdain has now been institutionalized in public policies that seem designed not so much to "save taxpayer dollars" as to punish and shame the poor. In 2003, the Bush Administration set out to crack down on "school lunch cheaters," children believed to be not poor enough to qualify for the federally subsidized lunches they receive ("School lunch 'cheaters,'" 2003); to require the thousands of poor peo-

---

[6]Rep. John Mica of Florida held up a sign that said, "Don't feed the alligators," and Rep. Barbara Cubin of Wyoming offered this denigration: "The federal government introduced wolves into the State of Wyoming, and they put them in pens, and they brought elk and venison to them every day" (Pear, 1995). In filing a bill in March 1996 to require mothers of children on welfare to identify their children's fathers or risk losing cash benefits, Gov. William Weld of Massachusetts remarked that some people seem to view parenthood as a "cheap joke" (Wong, 1996, p. B1).

ple who receive federal housing aid to pay more for rent (Pear, 2003b); and, through the Internal Revenue Service (IRS), to require the working poor who claim the earned income tax credit to provide "the most exhaustive proof of eligibility ever demanded of any class of taxpayers," with the likely result that many who should receive the credit will not even apply or will have to pay commercial tax preparers for help (Walsh, 2003).[7] In yet another blow, Congressional negotiators at the last minute deleted provisions in the sweeping tax-cut law passed in the summer of 2003 that would have allowed millions of minimum-wage families to receive an increase in the child tax credit along with other taxpayers. The exclusion means families of about half of all African-American and Latino children will get only a partial benefit, or none at all, from the increase in the child credit (Herbert, 2003c).

Along with all the other social ills dumped on the poor, blame too is "exported." In his now-classic book, *Blaming the Victim*, Ryan (1976) described the rationalization required to construe those who suffer the harshest consequences of social ills as their cause: "Typical is the swerving away from the central target that requires systematic change and, instead, focusing in on the individual affected. The ultimate effect is always to distract attention from the basic causes and to leave the primary social injustice untouched" (p. 25). We rarely hear of "victims" anymore. This consciousness has been crowded out by talk about "personal responsibility." But the deft shift-in-blame Ryan (1976) identified is evident today in policies that punish and shame the poor without addressing—as a way of not addressing—the social causes of poverty in concentrations of power and wealth and in a social system that serves that interest.

The next chapter looks at the demographics of child poverty in the United States and offers a critique of the official methods of counting the poor.

---

[7] According to IRS estimates, the U.S. Treasury lost $8.5 billion to $9.9 billion in 1999 by giving the tax credit to people who should not have had it. By comparison, according to study by a Harvard economist, corporations avoided paying as much as $54 billion owed in 1998. IRS records show one in every 64 people who claimed the earned income tax credit was audited in 2002, compared with one in every 120 taxpayers with annual incomes of more than $100,000 (Walsh, 2003).

5

Demographics of Poverty

No one would argue that being born into poverty is the fault of the child. It is merely the lottery of birth. And it is fundamental to shared concepts of progress and civilization that an accident of birth should not be allowed to circumscribe the quality of life. The poverty-bar may not be written into the laws and institutions of the land; but it is written into both the statistical chances and the everyday realities of millions of children who happen to be born into the poorest strata of our societies.

—United Nation's Children's Fund (2000a, p. 3)

When *The Other America* was published in 1962, readers responded with alarm. Harrington's documentation of widespread poverty and his call to action helped launch the set of public policies and programs known as the War on Poverty. Although there are those who argue that "the war" turned out to be against the poor, not poverty (e.g., Gans, 1996), for about a decade poverty was treated as a serious social problem. Thanks to Social Security, Supplemental Social Insurance, Aid to Families with Dependent Children, and other government transfer programs initiated during this time, about half the poor were lifted out of poverty between 1965 and 1972 (Katz, 1989).

This history offers a perspective on our own very different time. After the longest peace-time economic expansion in the history of the United States, an analysis of the Luxembourg Income Survey (Bradbury & Jantii, 2001) showed that the United States had the highest child poverty rate among 25 industrialized countries, with the exception of Russia. This ranking was based on a calculation of the percentage of children likely to be living in a poor family, defined as one with a disposable income of less than half the country's median income (the point at which half of all households have higher incomes and half have lower incomes). Using this definition of poverty, the

United States had a child poverty rate of 26.3%, compared, at the high end, with Russia's rate of 26.6% and, at the low end, with the Czech Republic's rate of 1.8%.

Wide variation in poverty rates over time and among nations at comparable levels of development suggests that child poverty is not an intractable problem. Nevertheless, it seemingly has fallen off the political map in the United States. The Children's Defense Fund (2002c) ranks the United States first among 25 industrialized nations in military technology, in Gross Domestic Product, and in the number of millionaires and billionaires, but 16th in living standards among the poorest one fifth of children, 17th in efforts to lift children out of poverty, and 18th in the income gap between rich and poor children. Reducing child poverty was not a stated goal of the 1996 welfare legislation. Neither has revising the now woefully low and outdated official measure of poverty been a priority—a topic to which I will return.

THE OFFICIAL PICTURE

First, consider what the official poverty statistics show. For 2001, the U.S. Census Bureau considered a three-person family poor if its annual income fell below $14,128. Based on this definition, almost 12 million children in the United States lived in poverty that year, roughly the same number as in 1980 (Lu, 2003). With a similar number in mind, former Senator Bill Bradley evoked this picture: If all the poor children in the United States were gathered together, they would make up a city bigger than New York—and "we would then see child poverty as the slow-motion national disaster that it is" ("Metropolis," 2000).

Who are these children who together could populate a city larger than New York? They are likely to live in a relatively small family, with an average of 2.2 children, and are much more likely to live in a family headed by someone who works for wages than a family supported by public assistance. Despite an economic downturn and joblessness among parents, in 2001, almost three quarters (74%) of all poor children lived in families in which someone worked at least part of the year, and more than one third (34%) in families in which someone worked full-time, year-round. Poor children in the United States are more likely to be White than Black or Latino and are more likely to live in a rural or suburban area than in an inner city. These probabilities are based on absolute numbers, however. Although more White children than children of color are poor, children of color suffer far more than their share of child poverty. Whereas 9.5% of all non-Hispanic White children lived in poverty in 2001, more than three times this percentage of all Black children (30.2%) and of all Hispanic children (28%) lived in poverty. Children in families headed by single mothers also are disproportionately poor. In 2001, more than 39% of all families headed by single mothers were poor, compared with 8% of all two-parent families (Children's Defense Fund, 2002a).

These numbers challenge the popular view of the typical poor child as a Black or Hispanic young person living in a large family in a central city. At the same time, the numbers show the extra price children of color and children in single-mother families pay in a society that tolerates such high levels of child poverty. By the year 2015, African-American and Latino youngsters are projected to comprise 60% of all children in low-income families—up from 47% in 1990, according to a study by the New York City-based College Board. The same study found that whereas one fifth of all children living in poor families had immigrant parents in 1990, one third are likely to have immigrant parents in 2015 (Olson, 2000).

Although a larger share of children in central cities than in rural and suburban areas are poor, 2.5 million poor children live in rural areas where rates of child poverty are often double or triple the national average (Save the Children, 2002). Of the nation's more than 200 persistently poor counties, 195 are rural. In four rural counties in South Dakota (Buffalo, Zieback, Shannon, and Todd) as well as Starr County, Texas, East Carroll Parrish, Louisiana, and Owsley County, Kentucky, more than half of all children are living in poverty (Children's Defense Fund, 2002b).

Of society's almost 12 million children living in poverty in 2001, about 5 million lived in "extreme poverty," meaning their families had annual incomes of less than half the official threshold (Lu, 2003). This represents a 17% jump over the number of extremely poor children in 2000. Almost 1 million African-American children lived in families this desperately poor in 2001—the largest number since 1980, the first year such data were collected (Children's Defense Fund, 2003). A study of young child poverty over the years 1993 through 1997 found very high rates of poverty and extreme poverty in the nation's largest cities: 44% of children under 6 in Chicago were living in poverty, 40% in Dallas, 58% in Detroit, 41% in Houston, 47% in Los Angeles, 42% in

New York, and 41% in Philadelphia. In several of these cities, most of the poor children were extremely poor: 60% of the poor children under 6 in Chicago, 53% of the poor children under 6 in Detroit, and 57% of the poor children under 6 in New York (Shirk, Bennet, & Aber, 1999).

WHAT'S WRONG WITH THIS PICTURE

These numbers, as alarming as they are, are based on an official definition of poverty as an income in 2001 of no more than $14,128 for a family of three—*and no one can believe this is all it takes to feed, clothe, house, educate, and otherwise care for three people, regardless of where the family lives*. By classifying only this level of deprivation as poverty, the official metric seriously distorts the hardship and suffering that come from having too little to meet a family's most basic needs.

Where did this way of measuring poverty originate?

> In 1795 ... a group of English magistrates decided that "a minimum income should be the cost of a gallon loaf of bread, multiplied by three, plus an allowance for each dependent." The poverty level today is set in much the same way. In 1963 Mollie Orshansky and her colleagues at the Social Security Administration set the "official" poverty line by using ... a "minimal diet—just sufficient to hold body and soul together—as the base." Since U.S. Department of Agriculture [USDA] studies in 1955 indicated that the average American family spent approximately one-third of its net income on food, Orshansky took a low-cost food budget prepared by the USDA, multiplied it by three, and came up with a "poverty line" for a family of four. And thus, the first U.S. poverty line was established in 1964 at $3,000. (Sidel, 1986, pp. 3–4)

The Office of Economic Opportunity adopted the Orshansky measure for its purposes in 1965. Four years later, what is now the Office of Management and Budget gave the measure official status throughout the federal government. The Census Bureau began publishing annual statistics on poverty in 1967 by comparing estimates of families' pretax income from its March Current Population Survey with the food-cost-based thresholds. The thresholds are adjusted each year for inflation, but not for changes in society's overall standard of living or consumption patterns. "Thus, the poverty line no longer represents the concept on which it was originally based—namely, food times a food share multiplier—because that share will change (and has changed) with rising living standards. Rather, the poverty threshold reflects in today's dollars the line that was set some 30 [plus] years ago" (Citro & Michael, 1995, p. 25).

Yet much has changed. The average family today spends a larger share of its income on housing, heath care, and transportation, and a smaller share on food than it did in 1955 when the original consumption data were collected (Citro & Michael, 1995). Still, a USDA report shows that the typical U.S. household now spends 36% more than the cost of the USDA's Thrifty Food Plan (on which the poverty thresholds are based) and "food insecure" households typically spend 4% more, yet cannot provide everyone in the family with the food they need for active, healthy lives (Nord et al., 2002). Also, many more mothers and fathers now work outside the home and so need to pay for child care. Overall, the officially poor are worse off today relative to the median family than they were in 1970 (Boushey et al., 2001).

At the request of the U.S. Congress, the National Research Council undertook a study of the official poverty measure in the early 1990s. The study group found the official measure to be "unacceptably flawed" (Citro & Michael, 1995, p. 21) and warned against letting "a key social indicator become so frozen in place that, when societal conditions change, it can no longer adequately reflect what it was designed to measure" (p. 43). That seems to be exactly what has happened. Although the Census Bureau publishes the annual poverty statistics, it has never been empowered to change the official metric (Citro & Michael, 1995). According to former Secretary of Labor Robert Reich, "The consensus [has been] not to change the standard for fear the poverty rate would look worse" (quoted in Uchitelle, 2001b, p. B7). Consequently, at the most basic level, we lack meaningful federal data on poverty. For purposes of determining eligibility for a host of social programs, we rely on numbers that almost certainly underestimate the scope and depth of poverty.

Other assessments of poverty exist. The comparison of child poverty rates in industrialized nations cited earlier, for example, is based not on the official U.S. metric, but rather on a definition of poverty as family income of less than 50% of the median in a nation. The challenge of defining poverty has concerned scholars for centuries (Andreß, 1998). Katz (1989) phrases the question well: "When we call people poor, do we mean they lack enough income to purchase adequate food, housing, clothing, and medical care? Or is poverty always relative, measured against contemporary expectations and living standards? Can we define poverty only when we know how most people live?" (p. 167). Ought poverty be measured against an absolute standard, such as income sufficient to obtain food, housing, and clothing, or against a relative standard, such as the ability to live in accord with social norms?

In rich countries like the United States, the latter probably requires at a minimum not only food, housing, and clothing, but also electric and phone service, reliable transportation, and child care for the large majority of parents who work outside the home. As Sen (1999) argues:

> The need to take part in the life of a community may induce demands for modern equipment (televisions, videocassette recorders, automobiles, and so one) in a country where such facilities are more or less universal ... and this imposes a strain on a relatively poor person in a rich country even when that person is at a much higher level of income compared with people in less opulent countries. (pp. 89–90)

The poor in wealthy nations, although relatively well off compared with the poor in other nations, may nevertheless be unable to participate fully in social life.

Recognizing the shortcomings of the official metric, organizations like Wider Opportunities for Women and the Economic Policy Institute have used alternative methodologies to cost out real expenses. Wider Opportunities for Women's Self-Sufficiency Standard has been used to determine how much money different families in different places need to pay taxes; to meet bare-bones needs for housing, child care, food, health care, and transportation; and to cover other basic out-of-pocket expenses. The standard assumes neither public subsidies (such as public housing, food stamps, Medicaid, or subsidized child care) nor private help (such as free baby-sitting by a friend or relative, canned goods from a food bank, or shared housing). A single mother of three in the Bronx would have needed $38,088 in 2000 to cover a no-frills budget even after tax credits, according to a study that used the Self-Sufficiency Standard for New York's five boroughs. This income is almost three times as much as the official poverty threshold for such a family and almost 60% more than a job requiring an average level of skills, experience, and education likely would pay.

The Economic Policy Institute (Boushey et al., 2001) has published budgets for various family configurations in hundreds of communities across the United States, based on what it actually costs a family to live safely and maintain a decent standard of living. The budgets include housing, child care, health care, food, transportation, and taxes, but not restaurant meals, vacations, movies, or savings for education or retirement. The budgets range from $21,989 a year for one parent and two children in Hattiesburg, Mississippi, an amount 64% higher than the official poverty line for the years 1997–1999, to $48,606 a year for the same family in Nassau-Suffolk County, New York, an amount equal to 362% of the official poverty line. Over the period examined, almost 30% of families with one to three children under 12 had incomes below the basic family budget levels. This included 52.1% of all African-American families and 56.3% of all Hispanic families. Half of all families with incomes below the family budget level included an adult who worked full time.

Calculations based on realistic family budgets suggest how grossly the official poverty thresholds distort the scope of economic hardship. Along with this criticism, poverty scholars have argued that measurements ought to account for the experience of poverty over time (Andreß, 1998). How long do people tend to be poor and how severe is the poverty they experience—that is, how great the gap between needs and resources? Is poverty generally experienced in short spells by many people or for long periods by a few people? Questions like these challenge the idea on which the official poverty measure rests—namely, that the population falls neatly into dichotomous categories of poor and not poor. In fact, when measures of the duration and severity of poverty are taken into account, a picture emerges not of "a dichotomy between the permanently, desperately poor and the never poor," but rather of a distribution of different experiences among the poor as well as between the officially poor and officially not poor (Walker, 1998, p. 39).

As always, the politics matter. The official U.S. poverty measure ignores in-kind benefits in calculating family resources, and so does not show declines in well-being due, for example, to cuts in food stamp benefits or to tighter restrictions on eligibility for Medicaid or Supplemental Security Income. The measure also ignores work-related expenses, such as child care. Because the official measure includes only two categories, poor and not poor, it tells nothing about the overall distribution of resources among the poor or about how some groups are faring relative to others. Consequently, "if income were taken from some very poor people to move a few less-poor persons out of poverty, the effect would be to reduce the head count, even though the depth of poverty had become worse" (Citro & Michael, 1995, p. 87). In 2001, poverty increased in both ways, in terms of head count and severity. Census data showed not only that more people became poor but also that the poor became poorer. The average amount by which poor people, including poor children, fell below the poverty line reached the highest levels on record (Center on Budget and Policy Priorities, 2002; the data go back to 1979.)

Because the official poverty measure calculates how many people were poor in a given year, not how many were in economic distress even if not officially poor, it obscures not only further impoverishment of the poor, but also the experience of all those teetering on the margins of economic insecurity. As Heclo (1994) argues,

> The "unofficial poor" may live beyond the official line most of the time, but they share the diverse insecurity of people, without much education, with jobs that do not pay very well or lead very far. They, like others, find their lives buffeted this way and that by joblessness, underemployment in a changing economy, illness that is uninsured or underinsured, day care that is a pastiche of unaffordable costs and improvisations, and any number of other problems. They need not cross a line to feel and be poor. (p. 420)

Because the official poverty line is calculated only annually, it tells nothing about duration, about the number of people experiencing either short spells of poverty or long, multiyear spells, or about how poverty affects households and individuals over time. Yet, taking duration into account alters the numbers significantly. Using the Panel Study of Income Dynamics (PSID), a longitudinal data set that has tracked thousands of individuals and families in the United States since 1968, Devine and Wright (1993) found that over a 20-year period (1968–1987), 11% to 15% of families were poor in any given year. However, almost 40% were poor (by the official measure) for at least one year during the two decades. "If one could extend this analysis over the average lifetime of a family, the proportion experiencing at least a year of poverty would have to increase and might easily reach or exceed half" (Devine & Wright, 1993, p. 105). This would mean "half the households in this affluent, postindustrial society are destined to spend at least one of their years beneath the poverty line" (Devine & Wright, 1993, p. 105).

Using the same data set, Rank (1999) found that by the age of 6, 57% of all African-American children are likely to experience at least 1 year of life below the poverty line, compared with 15% of all White children. By age 12, 67% of all African-American children and 21% of all White children are likely to be poor for at least a year, and by age 17, 69% of all African-American youth and 26% of White young people are likely to live below the poverty line for at least a year. By age 75, 91% of all African-Americans and 53% of all White Americans are likely to have experienced poverty at some point in their lives. These studies not only underscore the economic significance of race in this society, but suggest that living in poverty is a far more common experience than the official statistics imply.

Aside from the particular problems with the official U.S. metric, no income-based poverty assessment tells much about the pervasive disparities and deprivations that shape people's lives. Access to good schools, to health care, to reliable transportation, and to some measure of economic security; the ability to fulfill personal and family responsibilities, such as caring for children and other family members; the opportunity to gain the education and training needed to improve long-term economic prospects—all this is related to income and to income inequities, but cannot be wholly reduced to these things.

Along these lines, Boshara (2002) argues for a focus on assets as well as income, which offers a more complete—and disheartening—picture of poverty. "Lack of income means you can't get by; lack of assets means you can't get ahead" (Boshara, 2002, p. WK 13). Today one quarter of the U.S. population is "asset poor," meaning their net worth, including savings, home equity, and other assets, would enable them to survive at the poverty level for no more than 3 months. "Take away home equity, or just consider liquid assets, and the poverty rate jumps to nearly 40 percent" (Boshara, 2002, p. WK 13). The bottom 60% of the population earns only 23% of the nation's income, but has far less, only 5%, of its wealth. The bottom 40%, which earns 10% of the national income, has less than 1% of the national wealth (Boshara, 2002). Living paycheck to paycheck allows no possibility of building a different future.

In a society reluctant to confront honestly the consequences of poverty for children and families without adequate income to live decently—as, I would argue, ours is—it is perhaps not surprising that an income-based and deeply flawed poverty measure has primacy as an index of social health and well-being. Quantified and related only to comparable indices of years past, the hardship and suffering, defined as shortfalls in income, can be counted and in some sense then forgotten—counted and accounted for. Concerns with poverty are reduced to concerns with income statistics, which reflect nothing more meaningful than estimates of food costs and the relationship these costs once held to overall costs of living.

TOWARD A BETTER ASSESSMENT

Concepts and metrics that shed light on the consequences of deprivation and hardship in society without distorting the scope of the problem or stigmatizing the people behind the numbers could improve educational reform agendas. Documenting the demographics of hardship more accurately could provide a necessary, if not sufficient, foundation for thinking more clearly about how best to improve poor children's school experience. The official poverty measure is not helpful in this regard, as any reduction in poverty rates appears to reflect social progress, regardless of what a given level of income actually enables a person or family to do.

If more children were officially defined as poor, the rationale for narrow targeting of many educational programs, services, and funding would be challenged. The image of a few disadvantaged students in need is built into compensatory educational programs and services through the official poverty line by which target groups are identified. Connell (1994) describes the identification process and its consequences:

> Whatever the formulae used to measure disadvantage ... the procedure always involves drawing a cut-off line at some point on a dimension of advantage and disadvantage .... [T]he cut-off is always placed so as to indicate a modest-sized minority. This demarcation is credible because of the already existing political imagery of poverty, in which the poor are pictured as a minority outside mainstream society. (p. 130)

A more accurate documentation of the demographics of hardship would challenge this picture of a mainstream with a few deviants on the social fringe and, with it, the too-easy translation of perceptions of difference—poor versus not poor—into judgments of value—"good" versus "bad" students, families, schools, or communities.

Also, if the diversity among poor children was more widely recognized, poverty could be seen more easily as poverty and nothing more—that is, not as a sign of something else (Connell, 1994; Weissbourd, 1996). The damaging effects of poverty could be recognized, without assumptions about cultural differences or deficits, psychological or moral shortcomings, family inadequacies, or genetic handicaps. Such assumptions on the part of social policymakers, educational leaders, and even teachers all too often have led to rationalization of inaction or discrimination against poor children and not to efforts to educate them well. If the poor will always be poor, and always lag behind in school, why worry about them? This thinking has constrained too many young lives.

Where does this leave those of us concerned with issues of poverty and schooling? How can we talk meaningfully about material deprivation, disparities in resources and opportunities, and the related social and educational injustice when the official measure of poverty is so flawed? The difficulties are real, but recognizing the shortcomings of the available tools helps. As a proxy measure of educational need, family-income-based poverty statistics provide only the crudest measure of deprivation and no measure of its social significance. We have no choice perhaps but to work with what we have, a flawed measure of poverty that legitimates a "false map of the problem" (Connell, 1994). Still, recognizing the difficulty is a start.

Us-versus-them thinking is sewn into the fabric of our social life, embedded in our annual self-portraits in the form of census reports on poverty, and institutionalized in what are arguably some of our most compassionate programs, such as those designed to compensate for lacks and deficiencies in nutrition (e.g., school lunch and breakfast programs), in educational "readiness" (e.g., Head Start), and in school-level resources (e.g., Title I funding). Research suggests these programs do help, at least at the preschool and elementary levels (Natriello, McDill, & Pallas, 1990) and so ought to be supported and expanded. Still, such programs do not challenge the distribution of educational opportunity in any significant way. On the contrary, they lend themselves easily to stigmatization of the very children they are designed to help.

Better ways of assessing or exploring the relationship between economic deprivation and situations in which children flourish educationally could show not only where the inequities and injustices are greatest, but also how they are compounded and with what consequences for children. The first national review of the Chapter 1 program, predecessor of Title I of the Elementary and Secondary Education Act, showed that "the longer a child is in poverty, the more deleterious the effect on his or her educational growth" and that every year lived in poverty increases a child's likelihood of falling behind a grade level by 2% (Orland, 1994, p. 43). The PSID mentioned earlier found that although most of the children in the study who experienced poverty were poor for fewer than 5 years, 15% were poor for 10 years or more. The average income of these very poor children's families was only about half that needed to bring them up to the official poverty level. In sharply disproportionate numbers, these children were children of color. Although 60% of all the poor children in the study were White, almost 90% of those who were poor for 5 or more years were African-American (Corcoran & Chaudry, 1997). More research of this kind seemingly could shape educational reform agendas in meaningful ways.

I want to add two caveats to this discussion. First, as problematic as the official measure of poverty is, the annual statistics nevertheless provide an index of real suffering. As family income decreases, damage to children increases (Children's Defense Fund, 2002c, Duncan & Brooks-Gunn, 1997; Polakow, 1993, 2000)—damage that in many cases can be, and sometimes is, significantly ameliorated by "throwing money." As Weissbourd (1996) says, "It doesn't require a genius to ensure that children who have vision problems get eyeglasses or that children have clean clothes or adequate school supplies" (p. 16). Responding to problems like these requires no new data.

Second, although I have focused on some of the technicalities of measurement, the issues are not fundamentally technical but rather moral and political. A flawed measure of poverty stands as the official index of economic hardship not because a better measure eludes our collective intellectual grasp, but rather because the official measure does exactly what many people want it to do. It reflects a reassuring picture of a majority that is prospering or at least getting by, juxtaposed to a "less well off" minority, which, because of the way the population is defined and measured, appears fairly small, stable, and unthreatening.

The challenge we now face, I believe, is to look honestly at ourselves through a lens that offers not a fractured picture of "us" and "them," but rather a vision of the whole, however wounded. The wounds surely can be diagnosed and the whole body healed, but only with a level of honesty that comes with straight talk and meaningful numbers. With this in mind, the next chapter documents continuing disparities in school funding, with a focus on recent decisions by supreme courts in Arkansas, Ohio, New York, and Illinois, and on a case pending in California.

6

"Savage Inequalities" in School Funding

Surely there is enough for everyone within this country. It is a tragedy that these good things are not more widely shared. All our children ought to be allowed a stake in the enormous richness of America. Whether they were born to poor white Appalachians or to wealthy Texans, to poor black people in the Bronx or to rich people in Manhasset or Winnetka, they are all quite wonderful and innocent when they are small. We soil them needlessly.

—Kozol (1991, p. 233)

The most important question to ask is: Does child A, born into community A, have roughly the same opportunity for a quality education as child B, born into community B? For most industrialized countries, the answer is yes. For us, it's an embarrassing no.

—Fulton (2001, p. 14)

When Kozol published *Savage Inequalities: Children in America's Schools* in 1991, the book made the bestseller list and was widely reviewed and seemingly read. I recall attending a discussion of the book at a public library in a low-income, predominantly African-American neighborhood in Greensboro, North Carolina. "This is not news to us," one of the participants said. "This is what our schools have been like for years." This woman, like Kozol, spoke with anger and sadness about significant, ongoing disparities in public schooling—disparities that were not random, but rather clearly patterned, predictable, and consequential: In highly segregated schools, children in wealthier districts (mostly White) tended to get much more than children in poorer districts (mostly of color) of almost everything money can buy for schools:

nice buildings, good teachers, up-to-date textbooks, extracurricular activities in abundance, and so on.

Consequently, most children in wealthy districts like Winnetka, Illinois, Cherry Hill, New Jersey, or Great Neck, New York, enjoyed safe, sanitary, state-of-the-art school buildings; well qualified and adequately compensated teachers; and opportunities galore to participate in art, music, and sports programs. Many children in poor districts, however, faced years of schooling in old buildings badly in need of repair, teachers lacking full credentials or a series of substitutes, books that were outdated and often rationed because there were not enough to go around, and few extracurricular activities. Consequently, children in wealthy districts learned they are special, deserving, and full of potential, whereas children in poor districts learned "they are not wanted" and do not really matter (Kozol, 1991, p. 35). Kozol (1991) condemned the system of funding and oversight that allowed such injustice, which leaves a mark long past the time children graduate, drop out, or simply age out of public school: "The state, by requiring attendance but refusing to require equity, effectively requires inequality. Compulsory inequity, perpetuated by state law, too frequently condemns our children to unequal lives" (p. 56).

What has happened since Kozol's cry of outrage? According to the National Center for Education Statistics, average state spending per pupil in 2002 ranged from a high of $11,009 in the District of Columbia to a low of $4,769 in Utah (Park, 2003)—a gap of $6,240. For a class of 25 students, the difference is $156,000. For a school of 500, $3.12 million, and over 12 years of schooling, the disparity grows to $37.4 million.

Disparities in spending within states exacerbate the inequality among them. The Education Trust (2002) found that in 30 of 47 states studied, school districts with the highest child-poverty rates have substantially less state and local money to spend per student than districts with the lowest rates of child poverty. In New York, the gap in state and local revenues between the 25% of districts educating the highest percentages of poor children and the 25% educating the lowest percentages is $2,152 per student, the largest in any state. Between two elementary schools of 400 students each, "this gap translates into a difference of $860,800 ... enough to compete with elite suburban schools for the most qualified teachers and to provide the kinds of additional instructional time and other resources that research and data show can make a difference" (Education Trust, 2002, p. 2). Right behind New York is Illinois, with a per-student spending gap of $2,060; Montana, with a gap of $1,535; and Michigan, with a gap of $1,248. It is not necessary to show a direct correlation between funding and achievement to recognize the truth of Thurgood Marshall's assertion, written in dissent in a landmark school funding case decided in 1973: "It is an inescapable fact that if one district has more funds available per pupil than another district, the former will have greater choice in educational planning than will the latter" (*San Antonio v. Rodriguez*, 1973).

Funding disparities show up, among other places, in the condition of school buildings. A 1996 report by the U.S. General Accounting Office (GAO) documented the need for an investment of at least $112 billion in the nation's school buildings for repairs and upgrades alone. At that time, about one third of all school buildings needed "extensive repair or replacement" (p. 1) and about half needed some repair, with most of the problems in central-city schools (p. 18). Since then, the problem has worsened. In its 2003 update of its 2001 report card on the nation's infrastructure, the American Society of Civil Engineers (ASCE) reported, "Due to either aging, outdated facilities, severe overcrowding, or new mandated class sizes, 75% of our nation's school buildings remain inadequate to meet the needs of school children." The ASCE called for capital investment equal to about $3,800 per student and gave a D-minus for the overall condition of the nation's schools.

Averages and sum totals provide an overview, but do not tell the whole story. Many students attend schools in good repair with more than adequate funding. The students in decaying and inadequately funded schools in disproportionate numbers are students living in poor neighborhoods, who in disproportionate numbers are students of color and students with greater-than-average needs (Anyon, 1997; The Education Trust, 2002; GAO, 1996). The Education Trust (2002) review found that in 31 of 47 states, districts with the highest proportions of students of color have substantially less state and local dollars to spend per student than districts with low percentages of students of color. Again, New York has the largest gap: $2,033 per student between the quarter of districts with the lowest and the quarter with the highest enrollments of students of color. In its report, ASCE (2001) noted:

> School facility problems vary by location (urban versus suburban) and community characteristics (poor versus wealthy). Generally speaking, the largest portion of schools reporting deficient conditions are in central cities serving 50% minority students and 70% poor students. Schools in rural areas also tend to be inadequate.

About 70% of the students in the nation's 55 largest city school systems are African-American or Hispanic. Almost all these systems (92%) have poverty rates above the state average, and 85% have disproportionately high percentages of English language learners (Council of Great City Schools, 2001). Fewer than one third of the students graduate from many of these schools (Taylor, 2000). Graduation rates hovering between 10% and 20% are not uncommon in the Bronx (Polakow-Suransky, 2001). "Despite a great deal of rhetoric about the general failure of the public school system, the problem of inadequate schooling is more often not a statewide, but a local, overwhelmingly urban problem" (McUsic, 1999, p. 128). The problem continues in part, McUsic (1999) argues, because "no state has yet been willing to fund poor urban schools at a level that would (after discounting costs for special needs) finance a straightforward education curriculum at the same level enjoyed by the average suburban schools" (p. 130).

This state of affairs persists despite the fact that as of 2003, plaintiffs had prevailed in school funding cases in 25 states (Hunter, 2003). Recent court decisions in Arkansas, Ohio, New York, and Illinois, and a complaint filed in California offer a fuller picture of continuing inequities and inadequacies in school funding as well as what can only be described as gross neglect and abuse of many schoolchildren, generally children of color in property-poor districts. The sections that follow focus on conditions documented in these cases not because they are necessarily worst-case scenarios, but rather because they suggest what is happening now across the nation.

ARKANSAS: *LAKE VIEW V. HUCKABEE*

In November 2002, the Arkansas Supreme Court affirmed a trial court's finding the year before that the state's system of school funding is inequitable, inadequate, and therefore in violation of the state's constitution. These rulings followed an earlier one, in 1983, by the State Supreme Court, which found that "many of Arkansas' students were receiving only the bare rudiments of an education" and that the state's funding system consequently was unconstitutional. "Not much has changed since then except that nineteen classes have graduated from our high schools; practically a generation," the trial court judge, Collins Kilgore, wrote in 2001. "Too many of our children are leaving school for a life of deprivation, burdening our culture with the corrosive effects of citizens who lack the education to contribute not only to their community's welfare but who will be unable to live their own lives except, in many cases, on the outermost fringes of human existence" (*Lake View v. Huckabee*, 2001).

At the time, Arkansas ranked 50th among the states in per-pupil state and local spending, and, in prior years, ranked between 48th and 50th in teacher pay. The statewide testing program showed that only 44% of all fourth graders were proficient in reading and only 34% were proficient in math. Of the 53% of high school graduates who went on to college, 58% needed remediation when they got there in English, math, or both. One district had adopted an Academic Guarantee Policy for college-bound students. The "guarantee" promised the district would pay the tuition for remedial classes for any student who took a college-preparatory program, graduated with a 3.0 grade-point average, and still needed remediation in college. This proved to be the case for 24 students in the class of 1999. "At these levels, students will not be able to compete successfully with their peers from other nations. They will not be able to lead productive lives," Judge Kilgore wrote (*Lake View v. Huckabee*, 2001).

Although some school districts in Arkansas offered a variety of courses—including fashion merchandising, marketing, and access to classes at a local technical college—others offered only "the bare necessities of a curriculum and struggle to do so" (*Lake View v. Huckabee*, 2001). For example, according to court documents, Lake View, a high-poverty rural district in the heart of the Mississippi Delta, had one uncertified teacher for all the high school math courses: pre-algebra, algebra I and II, geometry, and trigonometry. The teacher was paid $10,000 a year as a substitute and earned another $5,000 a year driving a bus. The trigonometry course required graphing calculators, but the teacher had only four for the 10 students in the class, and no compasses for the geometry class.

> Only one of four chalkboards is useable. [The math teacher's] computer lacks hard and software, it has no sound chip, and the printer does not work. Paper is in short supply and the duplicating machine, an addressograph, is generally overworked so that frequently documents, including examinations, have to be handwritten on the chalkboard. (*Lake View v. Huckabee*, 2001)

Lake View offered no organized competitive sports except basketball, and still could not provide uniforms for the whole team.

The cumulative effects of years of inequities has left many of the poorest districts in need of far more than equal funding, Judge Kilgore argued. Buildings in the eastern part of the state are in particularly bad shape: "poor heating and air conditioning systems, broken and missing windows, missing floor tiles and walls in need of repair ... leaking roofs, asbestos problems, ceiling tiles ... missing and molded" (*Lake View v. Huckabee*, 2001). At Barton Elementary, more than 100 children shared two bathrooms with a total of four stalls. "An uneducated person has virtually no chance today to sample much more than a harsh subsistence," Kilgore wrote and instructed the state legislature to determine how much it would cost to fund an adequate education for the state's public school students (*Lake View v. Huckabee*, 2001).

The Arkansas Supreme Court affirmed Kilgore's decision in 2002, over the governor's appeal, and gave the state until January 1, 2004, to fix its school funding system. "We emphasize, once more, the dire need for changing the school funding system forthwith," Justice Robert Brown wrote and noted Arkansas's "abysmal rankings" in terms of high school graduation rates, standardized-test scores, and school spending (quoted in Gehring, 2002, p. 18). When lawmakers failed to act by the January 1, 2004, deadline, the Lake View district asked the State Supreme Court to shut down financing for the state government to force the Legislature to comply with the court order ("School district tries," 2004).

OHIO: *DEROLPH V. STATE*

Schoolchildren in underfunded schools in Ohio share many of the hardships of their counterparts in Arkansas. In May 2003, the Ohio Supreme Court said what it had said four times before: The state's system of school funding is unconstitutional. The court also made clear that responsibility for fixing the problem lies with the legislature, not the court, which leaves plaintiffs with no legal recourse if legislators opt not to change the state's school funding system. "It's like the court said, 'You are guilty but you are free,'" said William Phillis, executive director of the Ohio Coalition for Equity and Adequacy of School Funding, which filed the lawsuit, *DeRolph v. State of Ohio*, in 1991 (quoted in Zehr, 2003). At issue in the long and politically contentious struggle has been a heavy reliance on property taxes to fund schools, leading to disparities so significant that the state's highest court repeatedly found

Ohio in violation of its constitutional requirement to provide a "thorough and efficient system of common schools."

After four earlier rulings—three finding Ohio's school funding system unconstitutional and one ordering mediation, which failed—the Ohio Supreme Court in 2002 again directed the legislature to change the way it funds public schools. The 2002 decision came after an unusual ruling the year before when the court said the state's school funding system, although unconstitutional, could be constitutional if the state changed the methodology used to allocate state aid to public schools and increased its overall aid. A 4–3 majority characterized the decision as a compromise it could live with in the interest of bringing the then 10-year-old matter to a close. In a sharp dissent, Justice Alice Robie Resnick protested that the fundamental problem of overreliance on local property taxes had not been addressed, despite the court's previous directives. Justice Francis Sweeney, also dissenting, argued that a "thorough and efficient" system of school funding cannot be achieved in the absence of the provision of equal opportunity, which the majority was not requiring:

> At the end of the day, can we truly say that we have been victorious? ... Can we say that the children in poor, rural, or urban areas have been given the same opportunities as their peers who happen to be blessed with the good fortune of living in wealthy districts with a high property tax base? . . .The hallmark of a thorough and efficient form of public education is that it works as well for the least advantaged as it does for the most advantaged. The funding system advocated by the majority sadly misses the mark. (*DeRolph v. State*, 2001, known as *DeRolph III*, pp. 100–101)

The governor and legislature subsequently asked the court to reconsider its ruling in light of the economic fallout of the September 11, 2001, attack on the United States, which they said would make it difficult to find the additional $1.2 billion the court said they should invest in public schools over the next 2 years (Richard, 2001). The court agreed and issued a decision in 2002, weeks before a new term began, when two newly elected justices would change the court's makeup. "The consensus arrived at in *DeRolph III* was in many ways the result of impatience," Justice Paul Pfeifer wrote for the majority. "Upon being asked to reconsider that decision, we have changed our collective mind" (*DeRolph v. State*, 2002, known as *DeRolph IV*, pp. 2–3). Accordingly, the court once again found the state's school funding system unconstitutional and directed the General Assembly to enact a school-funding scheme that is "thorough and efficient," but provided no deadline or enforcement mechanism. It reaffirmed this finding in 2003 and made clear the case was over.

The saga of *DeRolph v. State* began in 1991 when a group of small rural and large urban districts, all very poor, filed a complaint that painted a horror-story picture:

> The Nelsonville York Elementary School ... is sliding down a hill at a rate of an inch a month .... At Eastern Brown High School, the learning-disabled classroom is a converted storage room with no windows for ventilation .... In the Dawson-Bryant school system, where a coal heating system is used, students are ... breathing coal dust which ... covers the students' desks after accumulating overnight. Band members ... use a former coal bin for practice sessions where there is no ventilation whatsoever. The Northern Local School District has ... been plagued with ... outdated sewage systems which have actually caused raw sewage to flow into the baseball field ... and ... arsenic in the drinking water. (quoted in Petronicolos & New, 1999, p. 406)

At the time, per-pupil spending in Ohio's poorest districts was approximately $3,000 a year, compared with $11,000 per year in much wealthier districts (Drummond, 2000). Twelve years later, in its 2003 review of public education, *Quality Counts*, Education Week gave Ohio a D-minus for resource equity.

As *DeRolph* illustrates, "Law books are filled with wonderful paper victories which have never been implemented" (Karp, 1995, p. 25). After a standoff with the state legislature in the spring of 2003, Gov. Bob Taft cut $90 million in state aid to public schools as part of a plan to close a $720 million state budget gap (Reid, 2003). When a coalition of school groups led by the National School Boards Association protested that the state had not fixed the constitutional violations, the State Supreme Court in the fall of 2003 declined to reopen the case (Hendrie, 2003).

NEW YORK: *CAMPAIGN FOR FISCAL EQUITY V. STATE*

In June 2003, the New York Court of Appeals, the state's highest court, ruled that New York must provide an opportunity for a "meaningful high school education" to all students and ordered the state, by the end of July 2004, to implement funding and accountability reforms to ensure that this happens for students in the New York City public schools. "Tens of thousands of students are placed in overcrowded classrooms, taught by unqualified teachers, and provided with inadequate facilities and equipment. The number of children in these straits is large enough to represent a systemic failure," Chief Judge Judith Kaye wrote in the majority opinion (*Campaign for Fiscal Equity v. State of New York*, 2003, p. 22).

At the same time, the court opted not to tie the practical definition of a "meaningful high school education" to the state's Regent Learning Standards. High school students now must pass a series of tests pegged to these standards to graduate. The court also warned other distressed districts not to regard its ruling as a green light: "New York City schools have the *most* student need in the State and the *highest* local costs yet receive some of the *lowest* per-student funding and have some of the *worst* results. Plaintiffs in other districts who cannot demonstrate a similar combination may find tougher going in the court" (*Campaign for Fiscal Equity v. State of New York*, 2003, p. 54). The court directed the state to ascertain the actual cost of providing a "sound basic education" in New York City and to devise a system to ensure that every school has the resources it needs to do this.

The Court of Appeals overturned a lower court ruling that said an eighth-grade-level education would satisfy the state's constitutional obligation and reinstated a 2001 trial-court ruling. At issue in the case was the adequacy and equity of the funding specifically of New York City schools, which for the 6 years prior to the trial-court ruling consistently were shortchanged in state-aid allocations and for more than a decade spent less per pupil than the state average, taking student need into account (*Campaign for Fiscal Equity v. State of New York*, 2001, p. 166).

Citing *Brown v. Board of Education* (1954) and its affirmation of education as "perhaps the most important function of state and local governments," the original trial judge, Leland DeGrasse, considered the broad context: What resources have been provided to the state's public schools? How equitably have these resources been distributed, and with what consequences for students? In a 190-page decision, DeGrasse documented inequities and inadequacies with respect to teacher quality, curricula, building conditions, and books and other supplies. The decision cites statistics for 1997–1998 that show almost 14% of New York City public school teachers were not certified in any subject they taught and describes school buildings in a "parlous physical state" after a "history of neglect" (*Campaign for Fiscal Equity v. State of New York*, 2001, p. 62). Documents in the case show that New York City public schools educate 73% of all students of color in the state, and 84% of all students in the city schools are students of color.

DeGrasse affirmed a "causal link" between resource-based "input" and "output" measures, such as graduation and dropout rates and standardized test scores; stressed the consequences of funding inequities and inadequacies for students in the city schools, a majority of whom "leave high school unprepared for more than low-paying work, unprepared for college, and unprepared for the duties placed upon them by a democratic society," and declared, "The schools have broken a covenant with students, and with society" (*Campaign for Fiscal Equity v. State of New York*, 2001, pp. 109–110). DeGrasse noted that fewer than 12% of all ninth-graders in New York City schools historically have received a Regents diploma, which requires passing scores on a series of standardized exams and which, with few exceptions, is now the only diploma available. Also, only half of all New York City public school students who started ninth grade in 1996 and stayed in school made it to the 12th grade in 4 years. Of the city's public school graduates entering the City University of New York, approximately four fifths have needed remediation—evidence, DeGrasse argued, of "a public school system that is foundering" (*Campaign for Fiscal Equity v. State of New York*, 2001, p. 101). DeGrasse suggested that although preparation for future employment ought not be the sole rationale for public education, high school graduates ought not be relegated to the ranks of the working poor. "While the greatest expansion in the local labor market might be composed of low level service jobs, such jobs frequently do not pay a living wage," he wrote. "A sound basic education would give New York City's high school graduates the opportunity to move beyond such work" (*Campaign for Fiscal Equity v. State of New York*, 2001, p. 23).

New York's governor, George Pataki, immediately appealed the trial-court ruling and initially prevailed. A panel of the Appellate Division of the Supreme Court reversed the trial court and argued that a sound basic education need not prepare graduates for "competitive employment," but rather only enable them "to get a job, and support [themselves], and thereby not be a charge on the public fisc." It added as explanation: "Society needs workers in all levels of jobs, the majority of which may very well be low level" (*Campaign for Fiscal Equity v. State of New York*, 2002, p. 13). The court suggested that students can learn to read well enough to land a job by the eighth or ninth grade, and that this level of education is being provided, even in New York City.

Advocates cheered when the Court of Appeals overturned this finding, but protested when Gov. Pataki shortly thereafter appointed a commission to consider how the state ought to respond. To them, this looked like a tactic to push back decisions about how to funnel more money to the New York City schools until after the next year's budget. The commission included no representatives from the Campaign for Fiscal Equity, which filed the suit. Meanwhile, state officials announced in September 2003 that more than 40% of New York City schools had failed to meet federal standards.

ILLINOIS: *LEWIS E. V. SPAGNOLO*

In 1995 a group of parents in Illinois sued the state and local school boards over the appalling conditions of the public schools in critically impoverished East St. Louis. The class-action lawsuit challenged not funding per se, but rather basic conditions. Plaintiffs cited dangerous buildings and schools without such fundamentals as teachers and books as evidence that state and local officials were violating the state constitution, which requires Illinois to provide "an efficient system of high quality public educational institutions and services." At the time, every student in the district was African-American and almost all were living in poverty (Jerald, 1998). Seven years later, in 2002, the student population was 99% African-American and 1% Hispanic, and 92% of the students were from low-income families.

Among the original plaintiffs was Anita Hicks, mother of twin boys in the first grade at Jackson Math and Science Academy. The *Chicago Tribune* (Grossman, 1997) reported:

> Hicks' disillusionment with her children's school began with the discovery that there was no teacher posted to the twins' first-grade room. Every time she asked why, the explanations changed .... "They were bringing in people off the street to baby-sit with the students," Hicks said. "There'd be days when no adult was in theroom. A teacher would pop in from next door just to check on them." ... When teachers were absent, classes were marched down to the gym to sit idle all day, parents charged. One group of 3rd graders had had, as their substitute, a sixth-grade student. (p. 1)

After a series of lower court rulings, the case landed in the Illinois Supreme Court, which ruled in 1999 that although the constitution requires the state to provide an "efficient" and "high quality" public school system, "quality" is a political question for the legislature, not a legal one for the court (*Lewis E. v. Spagnolo*, 1999). The court did not suggest that East St. Louis students were receiving a minimally adequate education, but rather that the problem was not its to fix.

In a sharp dissent from the majority, Chief Justice Freeman condemned the "intolerable and illegal conditions" in what, he said, had become "one of the worst [school] systems in the nation."

> Strangers wander in and out of junior high schools. Fire alarms malfunction, and firefighters find emergency exits chained shut as they rescue children from burning schools. Classrooms are sealed to protect students from asbestos and dangerous structural flaws. In dark corridors, light bulbs go unreplaced and rain seeps through leaky roofs. In heavy rains backed-up sewers flood school kitchens, boilers, and electrical systems, resulting in student evacuations and cancelled classes. Bathrooms are unsanitary and water fountains are dry or spew brown water. In winter, students sit through classes wearing heavy coats because broken windows and faulty boilers go unrepaired. They struggle to learn using meager instructional equipment and tattered, dated textbooks. School libraries are locked or destroyed by fire. Children never know whether they will have a teacher. (*Lewis E. v. Spagnolo*, 1999)

To the majority contention that the question before the court was an inappropriate one of politics, Freeman countered that plaintiffs were not asking the court "to enter the arena of Illinois public school policy," but simply "to do its job and interpret the Illinois Constitution" (*Lewis E. v. Spagnolo*, 1999). He also pointed out that the majority did not dispute the appalling conditions of the East St. Louis schools, but nevertheless did not "adequately relate the effect that these abhorrent physical conditions have on schoolchildren" (*Lewis E. v. Spagnolo*, 1999). Indeed, the majority opinion failed to address the consequences of the squalid school conditions for young people at all.

Not surprisingly, educational achievement in the district had been and still is low. Most of the students fail to meet the state's minimum learning goals, only about half graduate high school, "and many who manage to graduate are ill-prepared for skilled jobs, college, or meaningful participation in a democratic society," Freeman wrote (*Lewis E. v. Spagnolo,* 1999). The 2002 district report card showed that only 14.6% of the graduating class of 2002 had passing scores on the American College Test (ACT).

An oversight panel created by the state reported in 2001 that although the East St. Louis district had been "saved from financial 'insolvency,'" it continued "to be academically troubled and one of the lowest performing school districts in the state." The panel attributed problems to local governance and to a "minority population ... among the highest in any large urban district [that] requires many special services and unique approaches to the teaching program," and concluded that current funding is adequate (Financial Oversight Panel for East St. Louis School District, 2001). An Education Funding Advisory Board (2002) created by the Illinois General Assembly issued a report in 2002 that called only for minor changes in the distribution of state aid to public schools, which, it said, should create a "leveling up effect" (p. 17).

CALIFORNIA: *WILLIAMS V. STATE*

On May 17, 2000, the 46th anniversary of the U.S. Supreme Court's ruling in *Brown v. Board of Education* (1954), a coalition of civil rights groups filed a class-action lawsuit in California Superior Court. The complaint charges the state with reneging on its constitutional obligation to oversee a statewide school system that provides even the barest necessities of books, qualified teachers, safe and sanitary buildings, and functional toilets accessible to students. More than 60 students attending 18 "substandard schools" are named as plaintiffs. However, approximately 23,600 students attend these schools, which overwhelmingly serve poor students, students of color, and students learning English. Consequently, the lawsuit also charges the state with violating state and federal equal protection provisions.

Plaintiffs in the case are seeking neither a specific level of funding nor for the state to eliminate disparities in per-pupil spending. Rather, "This suit returns to the oldest state function, which is to provide a minimal floor of educational provisions below which no school should drop. In the early 1900s, the state's major role was to ensure that all schools met a minimum floor. They inspected facilities, looked at toilets, and worried about teacher credentials" (Michael Kirst, quoted in Sandham, 2000).

Because the allegations are so powerful, I have quoted extensively from the complaint, a 53-page litany of gross educational neglect. According to the complaint (*Williams v. State of California*, 2000), at Luther Burbank Middle School in San Francisco:

> Some math, science, and other core classes, do not have even enough textbooks for all the students in a single class to use during the school day .... The social studies textbook ... is so old it does not reflect the

breakup of the former Soviet Union .... [The school] is infested with vermin and roaches .... One dead rodent has remained, decomposing, in a corner in the gymnasium since the beginning of the school year .... The school library is rarely open [and] has no librarian .... Two of the three bathrooms ... are locked all day, every day. The third bathroom is locked during lunch and other periods ... so there are times during school when no bathroom at all is available for students to use. Students have urinated or defecated on themselves at school because they could not get into an unlocked bathroom .... The school has no air conditioning. On hot days classroom temperatures climb into the 90s .... In winter, children often wear coats, hats, and gloves during class to keep warm. (pp. 19–21)

At Bryant Elementary, also in San Francisco:

[One] teacher did not receive her math textbooks until February, in a school year that began in August. Another teacher still had not received half her district-mandated first-grade curriculum even after two thirds of the school year had been completed .... Teachers buy pencils, erasers, crayons, scissors, calendars, and maps so their students will have basic tools to use to learn .... The air conditioning and heat do not work in many classrooms .... Teachers have to spray students with water to keep them cool during spring, summer, and fall .... On cool days, students wear coats and mittens inside to keep warm .... The school has no nurse .... Water at the school is unsafe for drinking. Many children bring bottled water to class. (pp. 21–22)

At Wendell Helms Middle School in San Pablo:

One algebra class has no books at all .... Ceiling tiles ... are cracked and falling off, and the school roof leaks in the rain .... Students sometimes cannot use the gym on rainy days because the leaks cause dangerous puddles .... Toilets often do not work .... Most of the stalls in the boys' bathrooms are missing doors. The bathrooms only rarely have soap or toilet paper or paper towels. (pp. 22–23)

At John F. Kennedy High School in Richmond:

Students in many classes at Kennedy—including advanced-placement physics, advanced-placement English, geometry, and algebra—have not had a formal, long-term teacher for the entire year .... All the students in one advanced-placement English class have declined to take the advanced-placement test this year because they feel unprepared ... after having had no permanent English teacher for two consecutive years .... No student in any World History class has had a textbook all year. (pp. 23–24)

At Stonehurst Elementary in Oakland:

One class permanently takes instruction on the auditorium stage, while music lessons—complete with trumpets, clarinets, flutes, and violins—or school assemblies or other noisy activities take place simultaneously in the same auditorium .... The students who try to learn on the auditorium stage begin their school day at 8:30 a.m. and leave at 2:45 p.m., but from 9 a.m. until 1:30 p.m. every Tuesday and Thursday, music lessons run continuously in the same auditorium space .... Another class at the school was rained out of its classroom .... The roof leaked so badly that one third of the classroom was soaked in water, and the students had to move permanently out of the room because the fungus and mold growing from the years of leaking precluded students' return to the room. Since that time, students in the class have moved four times .... [Most recently] the students have displaced a special-education class to take instruction in a portable classroom designed to hold eight special-education students, not 30 fourth- and fifth-grade students. The portable classroom has only approximately 750 square feet, so the students are sardined together. (pp. 24–25)

At Cesar Chavez Academy in East Palo Alto:

Fifty-seven percent of the teachers lack full, nonemergency teaching credentials, and 76% of the students are still learning the English language .... The school does not provide teachers who have obtained even minimal teaching qualifications, much less specialized qualifications to teach English language learners .... Some classes do not have textbooks at all .... Many classroom lights do not work and some classrooms have broken glass in the windows .... The school has no nurse. When a child is hurt in an accident, the school calls 911. Parents then have to pay for ambulance and hospital care for children whose needs a school nurse could competently have attended. (p. 27)

At Mark Keppel High in Alhambra:

[There is] only one science lab that approximately 2,100 students must share [and] students ... must pay a lab fee for science instruction .... There are only approximately 15 [bathroom] stalls for boys and 23 stalls for girls in the entire school .... The school does not have enough space for all students to sit down during lunch period .... The [school] computer lab is equipped with computers that are obsolete by ten years and that cannot be wired to the Internet. The electrical wiring at the school is too old to power the computers without short circuiting, so computers regularly crash .... Temperatures have reached as high as 120 degrees in a class taught in a corrugated metal shed. (pp. 28–29)

At Cahuenga Elementary in Los Angeles:

> Overcrowding is so severe that the school has resorted to a three-track schedule for student attendance .... 83.7% of the students are still learning the English language, but 28 of the 65 teachers at the school lack training to teach any children, much less specialized training to teach children who need English language instruction .... The cafeteria where children eat is filthy. Parents have seen custodial staff wipe the tables with mops the custodians have used to clean the floors. (p. 30)

At Thomas Jefferson Senior High in Los Angeles:

> Students do not have desks at which to sit in some classes. Instead, students sit on counters or stand in the back of the room .... Some classes ... have no teacher at all. In one class, the teacher called in sick for five or six consecutive weeks this year, and students in the class wandered around the school during that period because they had no formal class .... The school does not offer enough courses for all the students, so many students spend one or two periods each day in "service" classes because neither academic classes nor study halls are available .... During "service" class periods, students try to find classrooms where teachers will allow "service" class students to sit quietly in the back of the room and do nothing, or students go to the main office and ask to run errands .... The school divides students into three separate tracks, with two tracks at school at any given time. Jefferson students receive approximately 20 fewer schools days of instruction each year than do students who do not attend multitrack schools. (pp. 31–32)

"These are schools that shock the conscience, schools where students can't learn and teachers can't teach," said Mark Rosenbaum, legal director of the ACLU of Southern California, one of the participants in the case. "These schools are the shame of California" (quoted in "Landmark lawsuit," 2000). Since originally filed, the suit has grown to include more students. Also, the governor countersued the 18 school districts, with the argument that local districts and not the state are responsible for school conditions. "We cannot have the governor out in our local school districts making sure there is toilet paper in all the bathrooms," said Secretary of Education Kerry Mazzoni (quoted in Gewertz, 2001). Proceedings on the cross-claims were stayed and the trial was scheduled to begin in August 2004.

Without the three decades of litigation over the equity and adequacy of public school funding, conditions conceivably could be even worse for many children in this country. Nevertheless, as in 1991 when Kozol condemned the "savage inequalities" in school funding, so too today many children still are condemned to "unequal lives," are "soiled needlessly" by the inequities, inadequacies, and shameful neglect that have shaped public schooling, and are learning that in the eyes of the broader society, they do not matter very much. As a former education commissioner in New York says:

> If you ask the children to attend school in conditions where plaster is crumbling, the roof is leaking and classes are being held in unlikely places because of overcrowded conditions, that says something to the child about how you diminish the value of the activity and of the child's participation in it and perhaps of the child himself. If, on the other hand, you send a child to a school in well-appointed or [adequate facilities] that sends the opposite message. That says this counts. You count. Do well. (Thomas Sobol, quoted in *Campaign for Fiscal Equity v. State of New York*, 2001)

More than 30 years ago, the California Supreme Court called education "the bright hope for entry of the poor and oppressed into the mainstream of American society" (*Serrano v. Priest*, 1971). Today, this ideal is undercut by denial of need and evasion of responsibility. For many poor children, especially poor children of color, schooling provides not even a minimum, floor level of opportunity, much less anything resembling equity or equality. As a nation, we have been happy to hail education as a door of opportunity open to any and all, but unwilling to in fact open the door for many children who need not empty promises and inspirational rhetoric, but good teachers, books, habitable buildings, and advocates with the skill and political clout to protect their rights. Proefriedt (2002) says it well:

> When it comes to funding the education of the nation's children, two principles are at work. The first, often enunciated ... is that we feel every child has the right to an equal educational opportunity. The second, almost never publicly enunciated, but effectively at work wherever funding policy is made, is that we do not wish to pay for the education of our poorer neighbors' children. (Proefriedt, 2002, p. 44)

The next chapter offers a very brief history of lawsuits over school funding and a perspective on the promise, limitations, and challenges of court-oriented advocacy for poor children.

7

No Guarantees: The Struggle for Educational Opportunity

Demography is not destiny. The amount of melanin in a student's skin, the home country of her antecedents, the amount of money in the family bank account, are not the inexorable determinants of academic success.

—*Campaign for Fiscal Equity v. State of New York (2001)*

We will increasingly see entire metropolitan areas and states where there will be no majority group or the majority group will be Latino or African American. This will be a new experience in American educational history. We will be facing either pluralism in school on an unprecedented level, with millions of whites needing to adjust to minority status, or the possibility of very serious racial and ethnic polarization, reinforced by educational inequalities, with the possible exclusion of the majority of students from access to educational mobility.

—*Orfield (2001)*

Decades of lawsuits and court rulings have left poor children with an uncertain right to educational opportunity. Overwhelmingly, it is the schools of poor children that are run-down or unsafe, lack adequately trained and compensated teachers, or have too few, if any, up-to-date textbooks. Educational opportunity for poor children has been shaped by multiple, often overlapping struggles, including African-Americans' struggle against segregation, Native Americans' struggle for self-determination, and immigrants' pursuit of the right to comprehensible instruction for children learning English. However, given this country's history of racial segregation and its practice of linking the quality of schooling to local wealth (by relying heavily on local taxes to fund public schools), educational opportunity for poor children has been shaped primarily by court-adjudicated conflicts over school funding and segregation.

These struggles, in many ways, are two sides of the same coin as schools segregated by race and ethnicity almost always also are segregated by wealth or lack thereof. Highly segregated schools serving mostly students of color are almost always schools in which most of the students are living in poverty, often in extreme poverty, and in neighborhoods in which poverty is concentrated. In contrast, schools that are highly segregated but with a majority of White students almost always enroll high proportions of middle-class students. "A map of schools attended by the average black or Hispanic student would almost perfectly match a map of high-poverty schools" (Orfield, quoted in Schemo, 2001). Segregation in schooling matters in part because poverty matters.

The strong relationship between poverty and educational attainment is even stronger when poverty is concentrated in a school (Kennedy et al., 1986). When the percentage of poor students rises above a certain level, needs become overwhelming, the quality of education often plunges (McUsic, 1999), and students of color pay the price. For all groups except Whites, racially segregated schools are almost always schools with concentrated poverty. Almost nine tenths of all schools serving largely African-American and Latino students have high concentrations of poverty (Orfield, 2001). This amounts to "ghetto schooling" for ghettoized children isolated by poverty as well as race and ethnicity (Anyon, 1997; Kozol, 1991; Ryan, 1999b). Many schools in major metropolitan areas are now both segregated and unequal in terms of resources as well as student achievement.

The discussion that follows focuses on three major U.S. Supreme Court decisions instrumental in shaping the educational opportunity of poor children in the United States: *Brown v. Board of Education of Topeka* (1954), which affirmed the fundamental importance of education in a democracy, the need to provide educational opportunity "to all on equal terms," and therefore the unconstitutionality of state-imposed segregation in schooling based on race; *San Antonio Independent School District v. Rodriguez* (1973), which found that education is not a fundamental right protected by the U.S. Constitution and consequently that a system of school funding that disadvantages children in property-poor districts is not necessarily unconstitutional; and *Milliken v. Bradley* (1974), which blocked efforts to integrate racially isolated city schools through interdistrict, city–suburban desegregation remedies, thereby all but exempting White suburban districts from participating in desegregation programs.

EQUAL EDUCATIONAL OPPORTUNITY AND *BROWN V. BOARD OF EDUCATION*

In the years leading up to the *Brown* decision in 1954, public schools were both unequal and racially segregated—by law in the South and in practice in the Northeast and West. Most of the school lawsuits filed by desperately poor Black plaintiffs sought equality of educational opportunity, but not necessarily integration. Families wanted something better for their children than the poorly funded, ramshackle schools that two thirds of all Black children in southern and border states attended. In 1940, public spending per pupil in southern Black schools was only 45% of that in White schools. By 1954, spending in southern Black schools was still only 60% of that in southern White schools, which in turn spent only 60% as much per pupil as the nation as a whole (Patterson, 2001, pp. xvi–xvii). The "Black schools" were often overcrowded, teachers were poorly paid, and students had to walk miles to and from school. Such conditions served the economy and politics of a Jim Crow South well. "When [Blacks] learn to spell dog and cat," many Whites believed, "they throw away the hoe" (quoted in Thernstrom & Thernstrom, 1997, p. 39).

The National Association for the Advancement of Colored People (NAACP), long concerned with education, had debated whether to challenge the gross inequality in educational opportunity offered to Black and White children or to challenge segregation directly—that is, to seek equality in facilities and resources for segregated schools or condemnation of the separate-but-equal doctrine affirmed in 1986 in *Plessy v. Ferguson*. Persuaded by Thurgood Marshall, who later argued *Brown* before the U.S. Supreme Court, the NAACP board decided in 1950 that from then on, "pleading in all education cases ... should be aimed at obtaining education on a non-segregated basis ... no relief other than that will be acceptable" (Patterson, 2001, p. 21). The goal would be an end to segregation in schooling.

The *Brown* case joined together five separate lawsuits begun by Black parents and students in Clarendon County, South Carolina; Prince Edward County, Virginia; the District of Columbia; Wilmington, Delaware; and Topeka, Kansas—courageous people who had come to believe that schools segregated by race would never offer the equal opportunity they sought. Although they ultimately prevailed, many of these plaintiffs paid a price for their efforts to secure something better for their children. Indeed, the NAACP struggled to find Black parents willing to join lawsuits, given the likelihood that workers would be fired from their jobs and their children would be attacked by White bullies on the streets (Williams, 1998, p. 98).

Levi Pearson started the case in South Carolina. A farmer and father of three, Pearson initially sought only buses to take his children to the local Black school, which, unlike the schools for White children, had none. The case initially was thrown out of court. Pearson subsequently was unable to find a White farmer who would lend him a harvester, and so lost his whole crop that year. The case then was expanded with more plaintiffs and broader demands: equality in buildings, teachers' salaries, and educational materials as well as transportation. At the time, Black children in Clarendon County attended schools that were seriously overcrowded and in many cases lacked running water, electricity, and flush toilets. During the 1949–1950 school year, the county spent $149 per White child but only $43 per Black child in the public schools. The total value of the 61 Black schools, which 6,531 students attended, was listed officially as $194,575; the value of the 12 White schools, which 2,375 students attended, was listed at $673,850. More than half the Black schools were "ramshackle shanties in which one or two teachers had only the most rudimentary instructional materials" (Patterson, 2001, p. 25). After a petition in the case was filed in federal district court, Harry Briggs, then the lead petitioner, and his wife, Liza, were laid off from their jobs (Patterson, 2001).

In 1951, 16-year-old Barbara Johnson telephoned the NAACP to say she had organized a student walkout to protest segregated schools in Farmville, Virginia. Two lawyers from Richmond went to investigate:

> At the First Baptist Church, they met with Barbara Johnson and a group of black students who took part in her walkout. "The students in Farmville had already gone on strike," [one of the lawyers] recalled. "They got 456 students involved in this, and they organized it, got everything ready. And didn't tell their parents or anybody." (Williams, 1998, p. 206)

The students wanted desegregation and not just a better school, Barbara made clear. The school's Black principal, who had nothing to do with the strike, nevertheless was fired for failing to prevent it (Patterson, 2001).

The issues were similar in Washington, DC, and Wilmington, Delaware. In DC, Gardner Bishop, a barber, protested when his daughter was barred from attending a White junior high school near their home and was required instead to attend an overcrowded school for Black students farther away. Black parents in the area supported a strike demanding equal facilities for their children. Later, another suit was filed on behalf of 12-year-old Spottswood Bolling, Jr., who had been turned away from a modern school with empty classrooms and sent instead to a dingy, ill-equipped school for Blacks. In Wilmington, Sarah Bulah's daughter, Shirley, was not allowed to get on a bus that went right by their house en route to an attractive, well-equipped school. Instead, Shirley's mother had to drive her two miles each day to and from a one-room schoolhouse for Black children (Patterson, 2001, pp. 30–31).

Rather than attend a school seven blocks from her home, Linda Brown, the 7-year-old third-grader and oldest child of Oliver Brown, the first-listed plaintiff in *Brown*, had to leave her home in Topeka at 7:40 in the morning, walk through dangerous railroad switching yards, and cross the city's busiest commercial street to board a bus that took her to a school that opened at 9 o'clock. Schools in Topeka, although segregated, were substantially equal in terms of facilities. This case was important, therefore, to force the issue of segregation as a matter of state policy, regardless of relative conditions (Patterson, 2001).

The *Plessy* and *Brown* decisions both turned on interpretations of the 14th Amendment to the U.S. Constitution and its equal protection clause, which states:

> No state shall make or enforce any law which shall abridge the privileges or immunities of citizens ... nor ... deprive any person of life, liberty, or property, without the due process of law; nor deny to any person within its jurisdiction the equal protection of the laws.

The *Plessy* court argued that the existence of equal, if nevertheless racially separate, facilities satisfied this clause. The *Brown* court disagreed and in a surprisingly unanimous decision ruled: "In the field of public education the doctrine of 'separate but equal' has no place. Separate educational facilities are inherently unequal." The court stressed the fundamental importance of education in a democracy and therefore the necessity to provide educational opportunity equally to all:

> Today, education is perhaps the most important function of state and local governments .... It is the very foundation of good citizenship .... In these

> days, it is doubtful that any child may reasonably be expected to succeed in life if he is denied the opportunity of an education. Such an opportunity, where the state has undertaken to provide it, is a right which must be made available to all on equal terms. (*Brown v. Board of Education*, 1954)

Along with this forceful affirmation of educational rights and the incompatibility of those rights with a system of segregated schooling, the court acknowledged that actually desegregating the schools would present "problems of considerable complexity" and agreed to put off the question of implementation for a year. When the U.S. Supreme Court took up the case again in what came to be known as *Brown II* (1955), it "clarified" that school districts should end segregation with "all deliberate speed"—a vague phrase that paved the way for decades of foot-dragging, noncompliance, and court-driven negotiation over what would constitute school desegregation. Arguably, agreement on this "compromise" of condemning school segregation without specifying how desegregation should be implemented enabled the court to reach its unanimous decision in 1954 (Patterson, 2001, p. 65).

Brown left a complex legacy. No longer segregated by law, public schools today are segregated in actuality by wealth as well as, still, by race and ethnicity. Spurred by the Civil Rights Act in 1964 and a series of U.S. Supreme Court decisions, the South made significant progress in desegregating schools from the mid-1960s to the early 1970s. The tide turned in the 1980s, and by the mid-1990s public schools in the South were more segregated than they had been in the early 1970s. Nationwide, the percentage of Black students in majority White schools peaked in the early 1980s.

Segregation in schooling intensified throughout the 1990s, despite the nation's growing diversity, including an increase of 254% in the Latino student population between 1968 and 1998. During the 1998–1999 year, more than 70% of the nation's Black students and more than 75% of the nation's Latino students attended predominantly minority schools (Orfield, 2001). More than a third of all Black and Latino students (36.6% and 36.6%, respectively) attended schools with few, if any, White students—that is, with minority enrollments of 90% to 100% ("School segregation," 2001). White students, the most segregated of all groups, attended schools where, on average, more than 80% of the students were also White (Orfield, 2001).

Nevertheless, through its strong affirmation of the right to equal educational opportunity and of the significance of education in a democracy, the *Brown* court invited further challenges to the inequalities in the prevailing system of public schooling (Enrich, 1995). As the momentum in the struggle to desegregate public schools stalled, lawsuits over school funding schemes became the primary vehicle for seeking equal educational opportunity (McUsic, 1999). In 1973 the U.S. Supreme Court faced a question very similar to the one Marshall and the NAACP had opted not to raise: Do gross inequities in all that money can buy for schools—decent buildings, good teachers, useful textbooks, and so on—deprive some children of the equal protection of the laws, in violation of the federal Constitution?

SCHOOL FUNDING AND *SAN ANTONIO V. RODRIGUEZ*

As the decisions and allegations reported in the last chapter suggest, significant disparities in per-pupil funding as well as educational neglect and outright abuse persist across the nation, despite the fact that almost every state has faced at least one round of school financing litigation (Cochran, 2000). Unlike almost every other nation, the United States relies heavily on local property taxes to fund public schools and in this way links the quality of a child's schooling to the affluence or poverty of the child's family and neighbors. Because the students with the greatest needs generally live in the poorest areas, this unusual and educationally unsound way of funding public schools almost guarantees inequalities in educational opportunity.

Funds for U.S. public schools come from federal, state, and local sources. The federal contribution has been about 7% of the total funding for public schools. States have been contributing about 50% of the total, and localities about 43% (Park, 2003). Among developed nations, only Canada comes close to the United States in the percentage of public school funds derived from local property taxes. In other countries, funding is much more centralized and therefore equalized (Koch, 1999).

The greater the local share, the greater the likelihood of significant disparities because property values and tax rates vary so much from district to district. Both variables, property value and tax rate, are important. Even if "property poor" districts tax themselves at very high rates, they will not be able to generate much revenue for local schools if there is essentially too little to tax. Contrary to popular opinion, disparities in locally generated funds exist not because poorer communities "don't care about education," but rather because school district property values differ so much. A study by the U.S. General Accounting Office (1997) showed wealthy districts in 37 states had more total funding (state and local combined) than poor districts, despite the fact that poor districts in 35 states made a greater tax effort than the wealthy districts — that is, taxed themselves at a higher rate.[1] The wealthy districts had an average of 24% more funding per pupil, even after adjustments for differences in regional costs and student needs.

School funding lawsuits, like desegregation lawsuits, grew out of the Civil Rights Movement and were fueled by a vision of equality before the law: If public schooling is provided for some, it must be provided for all on equal terms. In a landmark case, *Serrano v. Priest* (1971), the California Supreme Court ruled that "the quality of education may not be a function of wealth other than the wealth of the state as a whole," and invalidated California's system of school funding. Shortly thereafter, courts in Texas, Minnesota, Kansas, New Jersey, Arizona, and Michigan struck down these states' school funding systems. However, two years later, in *San Antonio v. Rodriguez* (1973), the U.S. Supreme Court held that disparities in school funding do not violate the U.S. Constitution, provided the system that produces the disparities bears a rational relationship to a legitimate state purpose. In this case, focused on Texas, the system was a method of financing public schools that relied heavily on local property taxes, and the legitimate state purpose, the preservation of local control of schools, which, in the mind of the majority, was linked to reliance on locally generated funding.

The case began in 1968 when Demetrio Rodriguez, a sheet-metal worker at an Air Force Base who had grown up in a migrant family, filed a class-action lawsuit with six other parents in San Antonio on behalf of their children. The children attended schools in the Edgewood district, which was very poor and 96% non-White. Ninety percent of the students in the district were Hispanic (mostly Mexican-Americans) and 6% were African-Americans. The elementary school building was crumbling, and the teachers, almost half of whom were uncertified, lacked basic supplies for their classrooms (Irons, 1988). Residents in the district taxed their property at the highest rate in the city, but local taxes provided only $26 for each pupil. State funds added $222 and federal funds another $108, for a total of $356 for each student. Meanwhile, residents of Alamo Heights, a predominantly White district and

---

[1]"Wealthy districts" were defined as those in the top quintile of district income, and "poor districts," as those in the bottom quintile (U.S. GAO, 1997).

one of the wealthiest in San Antonio, taxed their property at the city's lowest rate and still raised $333 for each student. The state gave slightly more to Alamo Heights than to Edgewood, $225 per student. Federal funds of $26 per student gave the district a total of $594 per pupil (Irons, 1988).

Plaintiffs pointed to such disparities in arguing that children in property-poor districts like Edgewood received an inferior education that amounted to discrimination. A federal district court in San Antonio agreed and in 1971 held that Texas's school funding system violated the equal protection clause of the 14th Amendment of the U.S. Constitution. Two years later, the U.S. Supreme Court reversed the decision. The majority of the justices acknowledged "substantial disparities" in funding, and Potter Stewart, in a concurring opinion, conceded that the Texas system was "chaotic and unjust" (*San Antonio v. Rodriguez*, 1973). Still, the court found the disparities constitutionally permissible because none of the children were being absolutely deprived of education, just given a lower quality of schooling.

The case involved two major legal questions:

- Is education a "fundamental right" protected by the U.S. Constitution? If so, based on the equal protection clause, the right must be protected equally for all, which would suggest the need for school funding to be more or less equal.
- Does wealth (or poverty) create a "suspect class?" That is, should children living in poverty be regarded as a group deserving special protection, given a history of unequal treatment and political powerlessness, much as, say, a group of children would be if denied educational opportunity on the basis of their race? Had the U.S. Supreme Court recognized poor children (or children in property-poor districts) as a suspect class, Texas would have been able to maintain a system of funding that discriminated against these children only if it could show a compelling state interest justifying the system.

Essentially, the federal district court said yes to both questions, but the U.S. Supreme Court—by one vote—said no. Among those objecting was Thurgood Marshall, who, in a long and passionate dissent, spoke to the moral and social issues raised when state policies deprive poor children of equal educational opportunity. The majority opinion, Marshall said, amounted to "a retreat from our historic commitment to equality of educational opportunity and an unsupportable acquiescence in a system which deprives children in their earliest years of the chance to reach their full potential as citizens." The right of every American to an equal start in life is too important, he argued, to be trumped by "grounds as tenuous as those presented"—namely, the assertion that a property-tax-based system of funding schools must be kept in place to preserve local control. Instead, he insisted, the state should bear the responsibility of ensuring equality of educational opportunity:

> The question of discrimination in educational quality must ... [look] to what the state provides its children, not to what the children are able to do with what they receive .... That a child forced to attend an underfunded school with poorer physical facilities, less experienced teachers, larger classes, and a narrower range of courses than a school with substantially more funds ... may nevertheless excel is to the credit of the child, not the state. Indeed, who can ever measure for such a child the opportunities lost and the talents wasted for want of a broader, more enriched education? (*San Antonio v. Rodriguez*, 1973)

Marshall challenged the finding that poor children do not constitute a suspect class with the argument that whether one focuses on the poverty of school districts or of families, there is discrimination on the basis of poverty:

> Discrimination on the basis of group wealth may not ... reflect the social stigma frequently attached to personal poverty. Nevertheless, insofar as group wealth discrimination involves wealth over which the disadvantaged individual has no significant control, it represents in fact a more serious basis of discrimination ... for such discrimination is no reflection of the individual's characteristics or his abilities. (*San Antonio v. Rodriguez*, 1973)

Particularly distressing to Marshall was the fact that the state itself created the disparities in funding:

> The means for financing public education in Texas are selected and specified by the state. It is the state that has created local school districts, and tied educational funding to the local property tax and thereby to local district wealth. At the same time, governmentally imposed land use controls have undoubtedly encouraged and rigidified natural trends in the allocation of particular areas for residential or commercial use, and thus determined each district's amount of taxable property wealth. (*San Antonio v. Rodriguez*, 1973)

Finally, on the matter of the alleged need to preserve local control, Marshall essentially asked, what local control? "Statewide laws regulate in fact the most minute details of local public education," he pointed out. If anything, a property-tax-based system of school funding limits the control that school districts, especially property-poor districts, have over their own affairs because "the quality of educational opportunity offered by any particular district is largely determined by the amount of taxable property located in the district—a factor over which local voters can exercise no control" (*San Antonio v. Rodriguez*, 1973).

Because the U.S. Supreme Court declined to give education the status of a "fundamental right" protected by the federal Constitution, *Rodriguez* essentially closed the door to using the federal courts as an avenue for school finance reform. Because the Court found disparities within states in resource-based educational opportunities to be constitutional, *Rodriguez* tacitly affirmed a system that was (and still is) largely separate and unequal (Burch, 2001). Without the possibility of appeal to the federal constitution, disparities in funding among states now stand as a given.

Although *Rodriguez* significantly hampered the pursuit of equal educational opportunity through school finance reform, advocates have continued to appeal to state courts, generally on the basis of language contained in state constitutions related to responsibilities for providing a system of public schooling. Less than 2 weeks after the *Rodriguez* decision, the New Jersey Supreme Court invalidated the state's system of school funding on the basis of the education clause in the state constitution, which requires New Jersey to provide a "thorough and efficient" education for all students. A funding system that allows wide disparities in per-pupil spending linked to local property wealth is not, the New Jersey court argued, "thorough and efficient" (*Robinson v. Cahill*, 1973).

In 1989, the Texas Supreme Court overturned the state's system of school funding on state, not federal, grounds. Citing "glaring disparities" and the "evident intention" of "the framers of [the Texas] Constitution to provide equal educational advantages for all," the court found the state in violation of the education clause in its constitution, which requires Texas to maintain a statewide system of schooling for "the general diffusion of knowledge" (*Edgewood Independent School District v. Kirby*, 1989). At the time, per-pupil spending ranged from $2,112 a year in some places to $19,333 a year in others, despite the fact that the poorest districts taxed themselves, on average, at a rate 50% higher than the wealthiest districts (Kozol, 1991). After the ruling was announced:

In the library of John F. Kennedy High School in the Edgewood district, Demetrio Rodriguez put his hand on his chest to fight back tears as students, teachers and community leaders cheered his vindication and their victory. As the crowd rose to applaud the 64-year-old man, Rodriguez spoke in halting words: "I cried this morning because this is something that has been in my heart .... My children will not benefit from it .... Twenty-one years is a long time to wait .... My children got caught in this web. It wasn't fair ... but there is nothing I can do about it now." (Kozol, 1991, pp. 225–226)

SCHOOL DESEGREGATION: *MILLIKEN I AND II*

For many years after *Brown*, school districts in the South stalled and generally did as little as possible to comply with the directive to desegregate schools "with all deliberate speed." In 1964 when President Kennedy asked Congress to ban discrimination in all programs receiving federal aid, 98% of all Black children in the South were in totally segregated schools (Orfield, 2001). Thereafter, spurred by the Civil Rights Act of 1964 and by several key U.S. Supreme Court decisions that required progress toward desegregation despite local resistance, the South slowly complied, as noted earlier. By 1970 public schools in the South were the most integrated in the nation. Meanwhile, in the North and Midwest where schools also were segregated by race, albeit not specifically by law, many large cities "were becoming holding pens for the poorest people of color in the country. A 'white noose' of suburban development was encircling them. And residential segregation, as always, sharpened racial separation in the schools" (Patterson, 2001, pp. 176–177).

The U.S. Supreme Court took up this situation in 1974, a year after it handed down the *Rodriguez* decision. The case involved Detroit, where an exodus of middle-class families had created an overwhelmingly Black school district in the city surrounded by suburban districts that were overwhelmingly White. Because almost no White people lived within the city limits, integrating Detroit's public schools was impossible. Lawyers for Verda Bradley and other parents in Detroit sought approval of a plan to merge the mostly Black urban and the mostly White suburban school districts into one metropolitan system that would allow for integration. Mrs. Bradley's son attended a school that was virtually all Black, badly overcrowded, and staffed by teachers who, "it seemed, had stopped teaching" (Patterson, 2001, p. 179). A federal district judge agreed with the parents and ordered consolidation of the districts. "School district lines," Judge Stephen Roth wrote, "are simply matters of political convenience and may not be used to deny constitutional rights" (quoted in Patterson, 2001, p. 179). A court of appeals affirmed the order in 1973.

However, when the case landed in the U.S. Supreme Court, the same five justices who had formed the majority in *Rodriguez* overturned the lower court's ruling. In *Milliken v. Bradley* (1974), known as *Milliken I*, the court acknowledged "disparate treatment of white and Negro students," but objected to an "interdistrict remedy" in the absence of evidence that the suburban districts had expressly intended to discriminate against students of color in Detroit. The court did not consider the role that suburban officials had played in housing segregation that virtually guaranteed segregation in public schools, but did express concern, in a familiar argument, about tampering with the "deeply rooted tradition" of local control (*Milliken I*, 1974).

In holding that a court could not order a desegregation plan that would involve the suburbs unless it was clear that suburban officials had intended to discriminate against students in city schools, *Milliken I* effectively let heavily White suburbs off the hook—and rendered *Brown* almost meaningless for most of the metropolitan North and West. Throughout these areas, city limits coincide with school district boundaries, with city schools serving largely students of color and suburban schools serving largely White students. If this situation cannot be altered, desegregation cannot be accomplished, as the Detroit parents realized. Together with the *Rodriguez* decision the year before, *Milliken I* virtually guaranteed that city schools would continue to be dominated by poor children of color and suburban schools by middle-class White children (Eaton, Feldman, & Kirby, 1996; Orfield, 1999; Ryan, 1999b).

In 1974 Detroit public schools were 72% Black. Detroit, then the nation's fifth largest school system, together with Chicago, the nation's second largest, educated more than half the Black children in the Midwest (Orfield, 1999). By 1986, Detroit city schools were 89% Black (Patterson, 2001), and by 1991, African-Americans were more segregated in Michigan than in any other state (Orfield, 1996). In 1998–1999, 90% of the students in Detroit city schools were Black, 70% were poor enough to qualify for free school lunches, and more than half did not graduate from high school.

Marshall, again dissenting, denounced the majority ruling in *Milliken I* as a "solemn mockery" of *Brown*'s promise of equal educational opportunity. "After twenty years of small, often difficult steps," he wrote, the court had taken "a giant step backwards" away from "that great end" of school integration—and away from a vision of a united nation. "Unless our children begin to learn together, there is little hope that our people will ever learn to live together," he warned. "In the short run, it may seem to be the easier course to allow our great metropolitan areas to be divided up each into two cities—one white, the other black—but it is a course, I predict, our people will ultimately regret" (*Milliken I*, 1974). "The wheel [has] come more than full circle since 1954," when *Brown* overturned a doctrine of separate but equal, wrote Justice William Douglas, also dissenting (*Milliken I*, 1974).

The U.S. Supreme Court sent the Detroit case back to the federal district court, and 3 years later, in what is known as *Milliken II* (1977), approved a remedy devised by the lower court: a modified desegregation plan, affecting only schools within the Detroit city limits, which also required the state to help pay for some remedial and compensatory programs. The *Milliken* decisions marked a turning point. With them, the goal shifted from integration to some form of reparations, for defendants, "a temporary punishment for the quickly absolved sin of racial segregation" (Orfield, 1996, p. 5) and, for plaintiffs, a last-ditch hope of winning funding to improve the quality of schooling at racially isolated schools (Ryan, 1999b). The question was no longer how society could realize the promise of equal educational opportunity for all, but rather how school districts could absolve themselves and return to the status quo. In a series of decisions in the 1990s, the Supreme Court essentially answered this new question and laid out a procedure for dismantling desegregation—one that, arguably, gives "separate but equal" another chance (Eaton et al., 1996) and allows states to buy their way out. "Termination agreements ... typically call for the dismantling of desegregation plans ... in exchange for a large, one-time payment from the state to the relevant schools districts" (Ryan, 1999b).

Court involvement in the desegregation and resegregation of the nation's public schools can be seen as a four-phase process: (a) affirmation of a basic right to equal educational opportunity in *Brown* (1954); (b) a decade of foot dragging and noncompliance at the local level, but also prodding of school districts by the federal government to move toward integration (1968–1973); (c) the *Milliken* decisions (mid-1970s), which shifted the focus to dismantling desegregation plans that had been put in place; and (d) a series of U.S. Supreme Court decisions in the 1990s that essentially offered a how-to procedure for drawing this project to a close. Decisions in *Board of Education of Oklahoma City v. Dowell* (1991), *Freeman v. Pitts* (1992), and *Missouri v. Jenkins* (1995) spelled out a process for dismantling desegregation plans and "established legal standards to determine when a local school district had repaid what the Court defined as a historic debt to its black students" (Orfield, 1996, p. 1). In fact, this can be accomplished fairly easily:

> School districts need not prove actual racial equality, nor a narrowing of academic gaps between the races. Desegregation remedies can even be removed when achievement gaps between the races have widened, or even if a district has never fully implemented an effective desegregation plan. Formalistic compliance for a time with some limited requirements [is] enough, even if the roots of racial inequality [are] untouched. (Orfield, 1996, p. 4)

If a court believes districts have complied with court orders for several years, they can send students back to neighborhood schools, even if those schools are segregated and inferior (Orfield, 1996). Consequently,

> By 1995 ... the announcements of resegregation and moves to request resegregation came almost weekly: Denver's court order was dropped. Minneapolis asked for an end to desegregation. Buffalo's court order was terminated. Cleveland's order was ended. Indianapolis filed for the termination of its plan. There was resegregation in Madison, Wisconsin. And massive battles loomed over some of the largest county-wide desegregation plans in Florida, Nevada, and elsewhere. (Orfield, 1999, p. 55)

In communities that have dismantled school desegregation plans, "the best evidence" so far shows "the rapid reappearance of extremely unequal schools for many nonwhite students" (Orfield, 1999, p. 42).

EQUITY AND ADEQUACY

Scholars generally characterize school funding lawsuits in three waves, based on the overall goal, equity or adequacy, and the violation alleged of federal or state law. The first wave focused on disparities in resources, challenged on the basis of the federal equal protection clause. *Rodriguez* ended this wave. The second wave focused primarily on inequities in spending or in the capacity to raise funds, challenged on the basis of education and equal protection clauses in state constitutions. The third wave includes lawsuits seeking some level of adequacy in funding or substantive educational quality, based on provisions in state education clauses.

Individual cases are almost always more complex. Equity cases, for example, may seek equity in funding or spending, in local districts' capacity to raise funds (that is, a promise that equalized tax rates will generate equal funds, with state supplements if necessary), in the quality of schooling provided, or in the outcomes of that schooling, such as test scores or graduation rates (Enrich, 1995). Adequacy cases, similarly, may be linked to differing standards—provision of the bare essentials of schooling (buildings, teachers, etc.), preparation of students to meet state educational standards, or preparation of students for competitive employment, higher education, or democratic citizenship.

After *Rodriguez*, many scholars believe educational adequacy arguments hold more promise as a goal of school finance reform than continued pursuit of equity (e.g., Cochran, 2000; Enrich, 1995), which can end up winnowing rather than expanding educational opportunity for poor children. Equal funding in the context of unequal needs disadvantages those with the greatest needs, such as students in overcrowded, racially isolated schools in impoverished central cities.

Equity in funding also can coexist easily with widespread inadequacy. The situation in California stands as a prime example. In *Serrano v. Priest* (1971), the California Supreme Court balked at the wealth-related disparities in per-pupil spending on public schools and overturned the state's system of funding. In 1974 a second court decision ordered the state legislature to come up with something better, and a new system was enacted in the spring of 1977. However,

> As soon as Californians understood the implications of the plan—namely, that funding for most of their public schools would henceforth be approximately equal—a conservative revolt surged through the state. The outcome of this surge, the first of many tax revolts across the nation in the next ten years, was a referendum that applied a "cap" on taxing and effectively restricted funding for *all* districts. (Kozol, 1991, p. 220)

In 1991, in 95% of California's districts, per-pupil funding varied by no more than $300 (Kozol, 1991), yet California ranked 46th in the nation in the share of its income devoted to public education (McUsic, 1999). California had the largest class size in the nation (Kozol, 1991), and the second lowest reading proficiency scores (McUsic, 1999). A 2003 ranking showed California 17th in the nation in the equity of its public school funding, but 48th in adequacy (Education Week, 2003).

Such educational sabotage has a history. Two decades earlier, voters responded to desegregation orders in the South in much the same way.

"Throughout much of the rural South, desegregation was accompanied by lowering the tax base for [the] public schools [while] granting local and state tax exemptions for [a parallel system of private white] academies" (former U.S. Commissioner of Education Francis Keppel, quoted in Kozol, 1991, p. 221).

Although equity has fallen short as a goal in school finance reform, so too has adequacy. If adequacy is defined as whatever it takes to enable all students to meet state learning standards, court victories based on adequacy arguments could significantly improve the quality of schooling for many poor children (Cochran, 2000). However, if adequacy means only a bare-minimum quality of schooling, victories could further legitimize a system that offers some children a much better quality of schooling than others. A system of public schooling that rests on no more than a promise of a low-level adequacy in no way ensures that poor students will be any better prepared tomorrow than they are today to compete for opportunities in higher education and the professional job market. Kozol (1991) explains the cycle well:

> Since every district is competing for the same restricted pool of gifted teachers, the "minimum" assured to every district is immediately devalued by the district that can add $10,000 more to teacher salaries. Then too, once the richest districts go above the minimum, school suppliers, textbook publishers, computer manufacturers adjust their price horizons—just as teachers raise their salary horizons—and the poorest districts are left where they were before the minimum existed. (p. 222)

If courts hold states to a standard of adequacy that amounts only to the most minimal level of educational opportunity, a system that reproduces advantage and disadvantage prevails unscathed.

STILL SEPARATE AND UNEQUAL

As the resource-based educational injustices documented in this chapter and the last one make clear, the ideal of equal educational opportunity has not been realized. On the contrary, the quality of schooling many children in property-poor school districts receive is neither equitable nor adequate, but rather demeaning, often dangerous, and usually racially segregated. Firestone, Goertz, and Natriello (1997) conclude their study of school finance reform with this sad assessment:

> The gap between the rich and poor districts in this country continues to be dramatic in both what students bring to school and the services they re-

> ceive when they arrive .... The litigation strategy has helped to minimize the damage to urban schools, but it has not bridged the gap between rich and poor. Twenty-five years of new court cases have generated stalled litigation and legislative steps forward followed by years of inaction with, at best, only minimal, often temporary, reductions in the inequities between rich and poor districts. (p. 165)

Some progress clearly has been made. After *Brown*, de jure segregation (by law) is no longer constitutional, and as of fall 2003, plaintiffs had prevailed in 25 states (Hunter, 2003). Still, many poor children, especially poor children of color, are back where they started more than 50 years ago when the NAACP debated whether to challenge inequality or segregation in schooling. Now as then, both are realities.

Many of the same lawyers worked on school segregation and school funding cases (McUsic, 1999). Lawyers challenging segregation in public schools originally sought to link the fates of Black and White students, and lawyers challenging school inequities and inadequacies, to link the fate of students in poor and wealthy districts. The idea was that "minority students would necessarily benefit from the desire of white parents and legislators to provide for their 'own' children" and that children in property-poor districts would benefit from the desire of parents in wealthier districts to spend more on their own children's schools (Ryan, 1999b). In both cases, however, the effort to link the well-being of some students to that of others seemingly has been abandoned. In school funding lawsuits, this disjunction happened as the objective shifted from seeking parity in spending to seeking affirmation of the right to a basic level of education, backed by resources sufficient to provide it. In desegregation lawsuits, the disjunction happened as the objective shifted from racial integration to a promise of compensation or reparation.

Progress toward the dream of equal educational opportunity will require an honest reckoning with the nation's history of racism. While some people hope and believe that the standards-and-accountability movement now sweeping the country will force courts to order states to fund a far higher level of "adequate" education for all students, others recoil at this prospect. "One of the things that really grates on people is that we're talking about pumping significant additional resources into large cities, and many people view those large cities as black holes" (William Duncombe, quoted in Koch, 1999).

Reviewing the outcomes of school funding lawsuits filed by predominantly minority districts compared with those filed by predominantly

White districts, Ryan (1999a) found that predominantly minority districts won only three of 12 challenges in which they were plaintiffs. This compares with a success rate of 73% (11 of 15 cases) for predominantly White districts, excluding cases involving large coalitions of districts. Furthermore, in the three cases in which predominantly minority districts prevailed (in New Jersey, Texas, and Arizona), the victories were followed by protracted battles with the state legislatures and repeated returns to court (Ryan, 1999a). In perhaps the worst-case example, the New Jersey Supreme Court issued more than a dozen school-finance opinions between 1973 and 2002.

Progress toward realization of the ideal of equal educational opportunity also will require owning up to the educational unsoundness of a property-tax-based system of funding public schools—a system continually justified as the necessary foundation of local control. The alleged need to preserve local control has given states a trump card in the face of legal challenges to their school finance systems and has allowed them to justify segregated schooling. However, as Marshall argued in dissent in *San Antonio v. Rodriguez* (1973), a property-tax-based system of school funding *limits* local control in many ways as local voters have no control over the value of district property.

A property-tax-based system of school funding protects privilege and advantage, but in no way assures that students' educational needs will be met. As Justice Alice Robie Resnick of the Ohio Supreme Court has argued, local property values have "no connection whatsoever to the actual education needs of the locality, with the result that a system overreliant on local property taxes is by its very nature an arbitrary system that can never be totally thorough or efficient" (*DeRolph v. State of Ohio*, 2000). As Comer (1997) notes, "The common argument holds that people at the local level know and care more about what is in the best interests of their own children. This argument is appealing, but in practice it is irresponsible. The record shows that the most powerful take care of their own and neglect the least powerful" (p. 179). Even it if were not the case that the most powerful historically have protected their own interests, why do we need local control when so little else is now local—not the job market for which all students presumably are being prepared, not the level of expectations to which all students presumably are to rise, and not the curriculum in these times of increasing standardization and test orientation? What in schooling, besides advantage and disadvantage, can reasonably be regarded as local?

Progress toward the goal of equal educational opportunity also will require recognizing that although money matters, money is not all that matters. Abandoning the goal of racial integration in favor of educational compensation remedies does not bode well for poor children of color (Eaton et al., 1996, p. 147). A short-term infusion of state funds to designated schools as "payment" for past harm cannot substitute for the far-reaching, structural changes required to address the lingering effects of years of racial segregation. When equal educational opportunity is defined solely in terms of money, the educational value of everything else—such as integration across lines of race, ethnicity, and class (McUsic, 1999; Ryan, 199b)—is discounted. Indeed, more money may be the cheapest Band-Aid of all. As in Minneapolis and St. Paul, Orfield (1997) suggests, so too in regions nationwide:

> Every few years, [the central-city districts in Minneapolis and St. Paul] threaten the legislature with a metropolitan desegregation lawsuit. In response, the education committees, with strong support from suburban members, approve increased funding for the city schools. Talk of the lawsuit then cools for a time. This ugly bargain is repeated in region after region throughout the United States. "We'll keep them here, if you send us money" is one of the most self-destructive parts of regional polarization. (p. 45)

Such "payoffs" do not alter the educational landscape for children subjected to the poverty and isolation of the nation's central city ghettoes. Teachers in segregated, high-poverty high schools, for example, are far more likely than others to be teaching a subject they did not study themselves. Also, when there are not enough students to fill advanced and AP courses, these opportunities generally are eliminated even for students who are ready, and the students then lose the special consideration many colleges give to their counterparts in other schools who have taken these courses (Orfield, 2001).

Overall, progress toward the dream of equal educational opportunity will require a broad commitment, backed by the energy of advocacy and a shared vision of basic fairness, to the social and educational well-being of all children. Court mandates to fund schools more equitably, more adequately, or both are not enough. As the last chapter shows, even when courts have overturned state school finance systems, state legislatures, charged with implementing the remedy, have stalled and procrastinated. Progress toward the provision of equal educational opportunity will require political courage and honesty about the injustices of our time, including the poverty, social isolation, and profoundly unequal educational opportunity so many children experience. Minimal compliance with narrow legal definitions of equity or adequacy or with temporary payments in lieu of desegregation is a poor substitute for the educational opportunity all children deserve. Although the highest court in the land has outlawed school segregation as an explicit state policy (*Brown v. Board of Education*, 1954), the fundamental injustice remains of segregated schools offering an inferior quality of schooling largely to students of color living in poverty. Today, this still breaks no law.

8

The Schooling of Poor Children

I don't think there's an educator who wouldn't stand up and say, "Poor kids have more problems when they come to school than kids who come from homes where they're not poor." It's so basic as to be—it's ridiculous that I have to repeat it. Yet as a country we want to come up with all these other things and say, "Well ... let's have another achievement test." You know, it's great to tell kids to pull themselves up by their own bootstraps, but you better put boots on them first.

—*Houston (in Hayden & Cauthen, 1998)*

If you want to understand the root of the achievement gap, it's the teacher gap that exists between the affluent schools and the less affluent schools. It's scandalous.

—*Haselkorn (quoted in Olson, 2003, p. 9)*

Poor children's experience in school too often mirrors their experience in the broader society. In disproportionate numbers, poor children not only are exposed to social and environmental toxins, and consequently suffer health problems, but also are assigned to the nation's worst public schools—schools in the worst state of disrepair (U.S. General Accounting Office, 1996) and with some of the lowest levels of per-pupil funding (see chap. 6). Children in poor communities too often end up in schools without adequate heating, cooling, or sanitation, and their teachers on the whole are less qualified than those in middle- and upper-class communities (Olson, 2003c; Prince, 2002; Wayne, 2002). Even lunch for poor children is not as good. Many school buildings in poor neighborhoods have no kitchen or, in some cases, even a lunchroom. Although children whose families are poor enough qualify for federally subsidized school meals, "the free lunch program offers students a prepackaged lunch that barely measures up to federal guidelines," said researcher Karen Evans Stout. "In affluent areas, the lunch is nutritionally rich" (quoted in "Lunch," 2002, p. 15).

Decades of research document the link between poverty and educational achievement (e.g., Halpern-Felscher et al., 1997; Kennedy, Jung, & Orland, 1986; Lee & Burkam, 2002; Orland, 1994; Payne & Biddle, 1999; Puma, Jones, Rock, & Fernandez, 1993). The link exists not because poor children cannot learn as well as others and not because "some families" or communities do not care about education. Rather, it exists largely because poor children are not given anywhere near the same educational opportunities as others, because public policy for decades has allowed poverty to grow and become so geographically concentrated it now overwhelms entire communities, including the schools, and because poverty takes such a fearsome toll on young bodies and minds.

> Poor families are more likely to move frequently for lack of rent money, disrupting school continuity. Children of jobless parents are more likely to encounter violence, alcoholism, abuse, divorce, and desertion related to joblessness and poverty. Poor children are much more likely to come to school sick, sometimes with severe long-term problems that limit their ability to see or hear in school. (Orfield, 1996, p. 54)

An analysis of the U.S. Department of Education's Early Childhood Longitudinal Study found significant differences in the cognitive abilities of children just starting kindergarten. Scores for children in the wealthiest families were 60% higher than scores for children in the poorest families—evidence of the multiple inequalities that disadvantage children "right from the starting gate" (Lee & Burkam, 2002). Of the factors considered (race/ethnicity, family educational expectations, access to quality child care, home reading, computer use, and television habits), the researchers found socioeconomic status "accounts for more of the unique variation in cognitive scores than any other factor by far" (Lee & Burkam, 2002).

"GHETTO SCHOOLING"[1] FOR GHETTOIZED CHILDREN

Research on poverty and education highlights the significance of family poverty, but especially of neighborhood or concentrated poverty—that is, of ghettoization. Because communities in the United States are highly segregated on the basis of income as well as race and

---

[1]The phrase "ghetto schooling" is from Anyon (1997).

ethnicity, concentrated poverty creates schoolwide poverty, which has even worse educational consequences for students than individual family poverty. When needs far outstrip resources, as they do in the poorest communities, which are also the most segregated communities, schools easily become overwhelmed.

Most, although certainly not all, of the highest poverty areas are in central cities in large metropolitan areas (Kingsley & Pettit, 2003). Throughout the 1970s and 1980s, poverty became more concentrated in particular neighborhoods. By 1990, almost a third of all Blacks lived in neighborhoods in which 40% or more of the residents were poor (Wilson, 2003, p. A19). Since then, both the number of people living in such economically devastated neighborhoods and the number of neighborhoods with this much poverty have declined sharply, but not across the board. In Washington, DC, for example, the number of high-poverty census tracts more than doubled in the 1990s, and the number of people living in these neighborhoods more than tripled. In the nation's capital, 24% of the poor now live in high-poverty neighborhoods (Cohn, 2003, p. A1).

The nation's 60 largest urban school systems enroll 30% of all African-American, Hispanic, limited English proficient, and poor students, but less than 15% of all public school students. More than three quarters (77%) of the students in these schools are students of color (including African-American, Hispanic, and Asian-American students) and almost two thirds (62%) are eligible for a federally subsidized lunch. Almost all these school systems have poverty rates higher than the statewide average, and most (78%) have higher percentages of English language learners as well (Council of the Great City Schools, 2003, p. viii). In 2000, in 86% of all intensely segregated Black and Latino schools more than half the students received subsidized lunches (Frankenberg, Lee, & Orfield, 2003).

Aside from the social isolation, concentrated poverty harms children in ways that make them more costly to educate than others. Even if per-pupil funding across school districts was equal, resources still would fall short in districts with many poor students, especially if the students also have special needs or are learning English or if districts must pay higher wages to attract teachers, as is often the case. In their study of school finance in New York, Duncombe and Yinger (1998) estimated that educational costs in New York City are 248% higher than the state average (p. A23). Given the disparate costs, depending on the district and student needs, "It makes no sense to expect a certain amount of spending to buy the same performance in every district" (Duncombe & Yinger, 1998, p. A23). Of course, as we have seen, funding is far from equal across states or districts, and those disparities, far more than students' or teachers' "motivation" or a community's support for education, contribute to gaps in educational achievement among groups of students.

Baltimore is a case in point. In 84% of the city schools, half or more of the students are eligible for subsidized school meals; in 60% of the schools, three quarters or more of the students are eligible. Yet, the city of Baltimore has considerably less money for instruction than its suburban neighbors—for a variety of reasons, including lack of property wealth and a large percentage of students with special needs, a challenge Baltimore shares with many high-poverty districts. In 1997, Baltimore ranked last among all districts in Maryland in spending per pupil for regular education and paid teachers less than their colleagues earned in surrounding suburbs (Orr, Stone, & Stumbo, 2000). In Baltimore's nonselective "neighborhood schools," 65% of the students entering ninth grade fail to graduate within 4 years (Delisio, 2002).

Haberman (2000), a long-time observer of urban education, argues that many distressed schools no longer function as schools at all, but rather essentially as custodial institutions. After researching the political and historical context of educational reform in Newark, Anyon (1997) reached a similar conclusion: "The positions of current actors in central city schools [are] almost unbearable" (p. xix). So too charged the president of the Los Angeles teachers' union: "We have kids without teachers, teachers without classrooms, and a district without a clue. The system is broken. Students and teachers are a forgotten priority in the poor city schools" (White, 1999).

Schools on Indian reservations (which are funded differently from other public schools) also illustrate what happens when the educational costs of deep poverty are ignored. "We got the worst of everything, the lowest test scores, lowest rate of reading books, the highest dropout rate, the lowest rate of entering college," said Dean Chavers, director of the Native American Scholarship Fund (quoted in Belluck, 2000). The high school dropout rate for Native American students averages between 36% and 51% and is the highest of any minority group. Only about 17% of Native American high school graduates go to college, and most of these do not finish. "Whatever test you're looking at, Indian kids in high school typically score at the 15th or 20th percentile .... Our Indian kids are leaving high school now with Algebra I—no geometry, no trig—and people wonder why they're failing out of college" (Chavers, quoted in Belluck, 2000). "We have schools that are literally falling down around the heads of Indian children," said David Beaulieu, director of Indian education at the U.S. Department of Education. "In the 1990s we had the same high levels of dropout rates and low achievement as existed 20 years before" (quoted in Belluck, 2000).

Omaha Nation Public School in Macy, Nebraska, provides an example. In 1999, the average student at the school scored in the 15th percentile on national standardized tests, and almost half the students scored below the 10th percentile. However, fewer than half the students in Grades 3 through 12 even came to take the tests. That year's graduating class of nine was twice as big as the graduating classes a few years before, but still represented only a third of the students who had started in ninth grade (Belluck, 2000).

"NESTED INEQUALITIES"

Inequalities in public schooling reflect a larger social segregation along the lines of race, ethnicity, and class. Hochschild and Scovronick (2003) speak of "nested inequalities" that shape students' experiences in school. The first "nest" is statewide; school funding varies significantly among states. The second is districtwide; funding varies within as well as across states. The third "nest" is schoolwide; even within districts, significant disparities can be found. For example:

> In Yonkers, New York, the subject of an important lawsuit over school and housing desegregation, schools in the city's northern and eastern section were built relatively recently and have beautiful grounds and excellent facilities; some schools in its southwestern section were built a century ago and have tiny playgrounds of cracked and slanted cement (or none at all) and dismal laboratories and libraries. (Hochschild & Scovronick, 2003, p. 23)

Finally, schools do not necessarily provide the same experience for all their students. Tracking and ability grouping persist, albeit under a variety of names, such as honors or Advanced Placement classes. Students in these classes receive a much different education than students in lower level, less challenging classes (Oakes, 1985). And so we come full circle: "Inequalities in family wealth are a major cause of inequalities in schooling, and inequalities of schooling do much to reinforce inequalities of wealth among families in the next generation" (Hochschild & Scovronick, 2003, p. 23).

The "nested inequalities" mean poor children are far more likely than others to have inexperienced or uncertified teachers, teachers without a background in the subject matter (Olson, 2003c; Prince, 2002), or teachers with relatively low academic skills (Wayne, 2002). A U.S. Department of Education (1999) assessment of the federal Title I program found teachers' aides, not teachers, were instructing children far more often in high-poverty schools than in other schools. Not surprisingly, these schools also have fewer computers with Internet access (Wong, 2000).

Nationwide, almost one third of all students in high-poverty high schools and more than half in high-poverty middle schools take at least one class with a teacher who did not even minor in the subject taught (Olson, 2003c). Qualified math teachers are particularly scarce in high-poverty schools. About 27% of math teachers in wealthy neighborhoods lack a background in math; in poor neighborhoods, 43% lack this preparation, Education Secretary Rod Paige told a group of teacher educators (Schemo, 2002a, p. A37). Fair pay and incentives could help close the gap in teacher qualifications. "It is a clear example of equal pay for *unequal* work if one set of teachers enjoys schools in safe neighborhoods, prepared students, well-qualified colleagues, and adequate materials in the classroom while another set of teachers faces quite the opposite" (Prince, 2002, p. 19). The result: "High-poverty schools suffer from fewer resources, greater teacher and administrator shortages, fewer applications for vacancies, higher absenteeism among teachers and staff, and higher rates of teacher and administrator turnover" (Prince, 2002, p. 16).

Consider the layers of inequality evident in Hochschild and Scovronick's (2003) description of two schools:

> In Newton North High School in Massachusetts, the students are mostly affluent and white. Ninety-nine percent graduate, 88 percent take the SATs, and 80 percent plan to attend a four-year college, 32 students were National Merit finalists or semifinalists in one year, and an additional 45 won National Merit letters of commendation. The school offers courses in 5 languages (as well as English as a second language), 14 Advanced Placement or college credit courses, and 34 fine arts courses. It has 3 student-run publications, 26 sports teams, and a wide variety of other programs ....
>
> On the other side of the country, [at] a school in San Diego ... 90 percent of the children are poor, 40 percent have limited English proficiency, many move frequently. A third of the teachers are brand new, and two of

> the twenty are out on "stress disability" leave. A recent evaluation of the school found that it needed a nurse, a counselor, facilities for parents and preschool children, and an adult literacy program. (pp. 21–22)

Such contrasts show not only the depth of need at many schools serving the nation's poorest children, but also the resource-based injustices that build on each other to shape the educational experience of all schoolchildren, affluent and poor alike, in profound ways.

TEST SCORES AND DROPOUT RATES

Although the overall quality of public schooling in the United States has often been misrepresented by those who would like to abolish the whole institution (Berliner & Biddle, 1995), public schooling has been plagued by society's failure to realize the ideal of equal educational opportunity, and that failure has had an entirely predictable consequence: Poor children are far less successful in school than others (Kennedy et al., 1986; Payne & Biddle, 1999; Puma et al., 1993).

Fourth-grade reading scores on the National Assessment of Educational Progress (NAEP) remained fairly even throughout the 1990s. However, scores of students in the bottom 10% declined significantly between 1992 and 2000 while scores of students in the top 25% improved, and the test-score gap between African-American/Latino students and White/Asian students persisted. The children with the lowest scores were disproportionately poor and of color. The 2000 NAEP scores show that almost half of all fourth-graders in central city schools and three fifths of all fourth-graders in poor families were reading at a level "below basic." The reading achievement gap between the highest and lowest poverty schools increased between 1988 and 1999, and in 1999 was equivalent to about four grade levels. The math achievement gap between these sets of schools also increased between 1986 and 1999, and in 1999 was equivalent to almost three grade levels (U.S. Department of Education, 2001). Such gaps have been "a disturbing feature of American schooling for at least 50 years" (Hirsch, 2001).

School dropout rates (arguably more accurately described as pushout rates) are highest in a few hundred schools in the 35 largest cities. Almost half of these schools graduate less than half the students who started as freshmen (Harvard Graduate School of Education, 2001). Dropout rates also are alarmingly high for Latinos: 31% for boys and 26% for girls (Canedy, 2001, p. A1).

Schools themselves bend and break under the weight of poverty. In most urban schools, academic outcomes "correlate powerfully with the percentage of low-income students the school serves" (McQuillan, 2003). One telling study showed well-off students in high-poverty schools scored *lower* on reading tests than poor students in mostly middle-class schools (Orr et al., 2000; cited in Hochschild & Scovronick, 2003, p. 26). The U.S. Department of Education's *Prospects* report (Puma et al., 1993) found a "tipping point" where poverty affects student achievement noticeably. Test scores for all students in a school, regardless of the level of family poverty, begin to drop when half or more of the students are eligible for subsidized lunch. When more than three quarters of the students live in low-income households, scores drop significantly (cited in Orr et al., 2000).

These statistics reflect shameful injustices in the distribution of educational opportunity. Access to college brings the injustice full circle, as young people who do not go on to college face the bleakest of job prospects and career advancement opportunities. More than three quarters of young people in well-off families go straight from high school to college; in poor families, fewer than half the young people follow this path. Students in well-off families also are more likely to attend a 4-year than a 2-year college and are much more likely to graduate (Hochschild & Scovronick, 2003, p. 79).

Nearly three decades ago, the United States set out to ensure that academically qualified students would not be turned away from college simply because they could not afford it. State legislatures subsidized public universities to keep tuitions low, and the federal government offered Pell Grants to the poorest students to cover most of the remaining costs. That social commitment is no longer evident. Public colleges, which educate more than three fourths of all students in the United States, are becoming unaffordable for many families. Between 1980 and 2000, tuition and fees at public and private colleges roughly doubled, after inflation (Arenson, 2003a). Federal and state financial aid has not kept pace with these increases. In 1986, Pell Grants covered 98% of the tuition at a public 4-year college; in 2002 the grants covered only 57% of the cost. Federal and state governments are moving away from need-based aid to more politically popular tax credits and other programs that shift public education dollars to the more affluent.

Low-income families in particular are borrowing more money than ever to pay for college, and many of the financially neediest students are opting not to even apply. The college-attendance gap between high-

and low-income students has widened in recent years. According to a report by the National Center for Public Policy and Higher Education (*Losing Ground*, 2002), about 25% of high-achieving low-income students are not going to college. As *The New York Times* (2002) warns, "Unless the country renews its commitment to helping the poor and working-class students get to and through college, upward mobility for tens of millions of Americans will effectively cease" ("Public colleges," p. WK 14).

CLASSROOM LANDSCAPES OF ABUSE AND NEGLECT [2]

No one's school experience can be reduced to his or her family income. Just as schools in wealthy communities are not always "good," schools in poor communities are not always "bad." Many high-poverty schools offer wonderful experiences for students who thrive in remarkable ways. But this is largely in spite of the social forces pushing in the opposite direction, not because poverty does not matter. The success stories attest to the dedication and skills of teachers, students, and families alike, and ought never to be regarded as a reason to overlook the glaring injustices that make them so inspirational. Such stories—"generally signaled by a standard set of headlines ('FROM THE ASHES: A FLAME OF HOPE')"—can be consoling, but "may permit us also to congratulate ourselves too easily about the 'bootstrap' possibilities for individual endeavor or for localized renewal efforts in an atmosphere where the toxicity of life is nearly universal" (Kozol, 1995, p. 162).

Most instructive, I believe, are the stories that show where society has failed its children and what change therefore is most urgently needed. Like Dickens' Scrooge who had to look honestly at the misery he was causing in order to change, society must own up to what its social and educational policies and practices are doing to far too many poor children. Observations of the abuse that poor children and youth experience in their schools and classrooms fill the literature (e.g., see Anyon, 1997; Kozol, 1991; Orel, 2003; Orenstein, 1994; Polakow, 1993; and Valenzuela, 1999).

Consider, as one example, the classroom life of 7-year-old Heather, reported by Polakow (1993). "Easy to identify as a problem sec-

[2]Polakow (1993) uses the metaphor of a "landscape of otherness" (p. 2) throughout her book *Lives on the Edge: Single Mothers and their Children in the Other America* to capture the experience of single mothers and their children living in poverty in the United States.

ond-grader as she sat at her desk pushed out into the hallway," Heather had been told not to speak to anyone and classmates had been told not to speak to her. Neither was she allowed to go to recess or eat lunch in the cafeteria with others. According to her teacher, Mrs. Mack, "This child just does not know the difference between right and wrong—she absolutely does not belong in a normal classroom with normal children" (p. 138). Polakow (1993) reports:

> I look at Heather, now being sent to the principal's office, awkwardly slipping in her flipflops three sizes too big for her, walking down the corridor—in the middle of a snowy December—dressed in a summer blouse several sizes too small and a long flimsy skirt. What had Heather done? "I've given up on this child—she's socially dysfunctional—three times now we've caught her stealing free lunch and storing it in her desk to take home!" her teacher said. (p. 138)

Heather lived with her sister and mother in a trailer park and often seemed hungry, especially at the end of the month when the family's food stamps ran out. "Apparently Heather had been caught stealing extra free lunch on three Fridays, knowing that she and her sister would have to wait until Monday for their next free meals" (Polakow, 1993, p. 138). Heather's teacher tried repeatedly to have Heather removed from the class and was angry with Heather's mother, who had refused to have her tested for learning disabilities. From the mother's perspective:

> Ever since I became separated and we moved here and applied for free lunches, you know, I've had nothing but problems with this school, and now with this teacher—she's always thinking there is something wrong with Heather. I don't see it; I told them I'd help Heather if they told me what to do, but they keep insisting I sign the papers. I told them I would not sign those papers, and they said if I don't sign the papers they would fail Heather. Now I don't know what to do. (p. 139)

Eventually tested and assigned to special education, Heather then was pulled out of class each day. Again, Polakow (1993) reports:

> The children are doing math worksheets, and Heather is sitting away from the grouped desks because "she always falls behind." About ten minutes into the math period, a teacher walks into the room. "Heather has to go with Mrs. King," announces Jan. "Jan, thank you, I'll tell Heather what she has to do," responds Mrs. Mack, signaling to Heather to leave. Heather is taken out and goes to the special education room for remedial reading. When she returns, math is over, and the children begin a social

> studies unit about Japan. "Sit down and pay attention so you can make up what you missed," says Mrs. Mack. Heather stands looking lost next to her desk as the children are busy gathering papers. She has to miss recess so as to make up her lost social studies time, and never does get back to her math sheet that day. (p. 139).

Although Heather was able to read, neither her regular reading group, the lowest in the class, nor her remedial reading class included any actual reading assignments. When she struggles in math because she is pulled out of class so much and never has time to finish assignments, the teacher reports Heather's "poor work habits" to her mother (Polakow, 1993, p. 139). Shunned by her classmates and targeted by her teacher, Heather's life in school is miserable. Polakow (1993) observes:

> Today Heather returns from the resource room to a desk piled high with the morning's work. Mrs. Mack tells her, "You'll have to do your work during lunch and recess because going to the resource room isn't a special privilege." I stayed with Heather at recess and looked at her work. Three of the papers were without errors, but the teacher had only written a small "OK" at the top. By contrast, I noticed that the papers correctly completed by other children had smiley faces and "good job" written on them. Heather's other papers, which had errors, were marked with large check marks and negative comments .... [Heather] feels marginalized by her teacher and her classmates and is very self-conscious about her appearance. She tells me that "Mrs. Mack always picks on me and I hate her ... I hate this school and I don't got no friends here." (pp. 139–140)

In her teacher's eyes, "Heather has no positive potential" (p. 140).

Such educational abuse neither characterizes the schooling of all poor children nor represents a single worst-case situation. Rather, it reveals a larger "landscape of condemnation" that shapes the lives of poor children in and outside schools (Polakow, 1993, p. 146). Outside school, destitution constrains Heather's world; inside school, she experiences humiliation and abuse. In her teacher's eyes, "Heather has no positive potential" (Polakow, 1993, p. 140).

Heather is not alone. "At Taft High School in the Bronx, one of the grimmest schools in the United States, the self-esteem of children has been crushed to the degree that students ridicule themselves ... by making a bitter joke out of the letters of the school's name. 'Taft,' they say, means 'Training Animals for Tomorrow'" (Kozol, 1995, p. 152). Here too, young people have learned what they are taught in school as in society: You don't matter; the opportunities this land offers are not for you.

Far more common than outright educational abuse, I suspect, are the misguided policy and practice and the inability to respond well to student need that I observed in a fairly high-poverty high school in a small city in upstate New York. Here are some entries from a journal I kept during my time at the school during the fall 2000 semester, primarily in the classroom of a remedial reading teacher I will call Linda.[3]

> Linda told me Lucia's father was murdered—chopped to pieces—in Mexico when she and her sister were little. The mother subsequently came to the U.S. The girls stayed with their grandmother in Mexico until their mother sent for them. Lucia did well her first year at the high school when she was considered to be in ninth grade. However, the next year, when she was then 20 years old, she was jumped up to the 12th grade and needed to pass 11th and 12th grade English, plus gym, to graduate. She cuts all these classes frequently, often spending the time in Linda's class. This annoys [a school administrator] who is trying to kick her out of the school. "Lucia is not doing well," Linda told me, "but it's because she was moved up so quickly. She doesn't go to class because she doesn't understand what's going on. If she drops out, her mother will have her start working. She'll end up as a maid or washing dishes somewhere."
>
> ***
>
> Asked to reflect on his progress over the course of the semester, Robert, a native English speaker in the reading class, wrote in his journal: "Think I try hard, but no hard enuf. I think that I was absint too much. I sould gone after school to make assiments. I should did my homework. It was just a bad time period, with my uncle leven, staying home to woch my sister, my necis. I didn't go outside realy. By time I do I am tiyer out. Next quarter I plan to work to my ultimed potential. I would stay as long more days than last quarter. Do homework, but if I had to woch somebody I will, but my uncle is coming back tomorrow on Friday. He is coming back so everything is going back to normal."
>
> ***
>
> Miguel, in the 11th grade, often comes for help during his lunch period. He is completely lost, especially in math. Today as we worked on some problems together, he grabbed the calculator to subtract 2 from 100. That didn't help, however, because he does not know the function symbols: +, –, ×. He cannot subtract 2 from 100 with or without a calculator.

---

[3]I have changed all names in the journal entries.

***

> Maria, 18, recently moved from Mexico to upstate New York with her mother and stepfather. For the family to survive, everyone has to work. Maria is working eight-hour shifts at a McDonald's after full days at school. She studied computer programming in Mexico, but now is trying to learn enough English to pass the Regents [New York's high-stakes high school exit exams].

At the end of her third semester, Maria placed in the third percentile on a national reading test. A diligent student, she nevertheless often came to school exhausted and was unable to participate in after-school homework programs because she went straight to work. This school, like many others, is overwhelmed by the challenges it faces: widespread poverty, students who arrive in high school barely able to read and write, learning disabilities that have been misdiagnosed as lack of English proficiency, and the enormous challenge of helping high school students who speak very little English acquire an academic-level proficiency in a year or two with no more than a few hours of instruction each day in English as a Second Language.

Too often, schools and classrooms offer poor children not a space in which to encounter new ideas and explore their creative potential in an atmosphere of support and affirmation, but rather "landscapes of condemnation" (Polakow, 1993, p. 146). Schools and classrooms become places where too many poor children learn that they do not matter much. As Kozol (in Hayden & Cauthern, 1998) suggests, this can—should—be seen as theft that cannot somehow later be made right: "There's no way to atone for the theft of childhood. No one can return your fifth-grade year to you. Once it's gone, it's gone forever." While so many other concerns take priority in the broader society, the losses pile up, child after child, young person after young person.

9

Educational Reform

The central irony of the "No Child Left Behind" Act of 2001 and related state laws is that they assure that many children will, in fact, be left behind. In Massachusetts, for example, 10% of this year's seniors [class of 2003] will not graduate with their classes (if at all) because they have failed the state's MCAS exam five times—even though they have completed all other graduation requirements. Last year, these 6,000 students would have graduated. The logic of this approach, if not the scale, is reminiscent of that famous comment from the Vietnam War, in which an official was quoted as saying, "It became necessary to destroy the village in order to save it."

—Gratz (2003, p. 36)

In all our stringent calls for "accountability," do we ever consider that maybe we as members of a society ought to hold ourselves more accountable for all of our children?

—Ryan (2001, p. 16)

With the No Child Left Behind Act, signed into law in early 2002, the Bush Administration put its stamp on the central federal law governing K–12 schooling, the Elementary and Secondary Education Act (ESEA) enacted in 1965. During his campaign for the presidency, Bush hailed the ideas that are now law as a way to improve public education across the board, especially for poor children. Vowing to end "the soft bigotry of low expectations" that he said has allowed too many poor children to fall permanently behind in school (Sterngold, 1999), President Bush declared, "It's time to come together to get it (educational reform) done so that we can truthfully say in America, 'No child will be left behind, not one single child'" ("Excerpt," 2001, p. A14).

Defined in this way, the problem of "low expectations" suggests the solution presumably built into the provisions of No Child Left Behind: higher expectations. However, the law requires not higher expectations—which, after all, cannot be legislated—but rather documented success, across the board and against a set of external standards. *Expecting* every child to succeed is one thing; *requiring* that success is another (Gratz, 2003).

Supporters regard the No Child Left Behind Act as a much-needed push in the right direction: a set of measures that will drive broad gains in student achievement and hold states and schools appropriately accountable for student progress. A number of critics see it essentially as a disingenuous set of demands, framed in an appealing language of expectations, that will force schools to fail on a scale large enough to rationalize shifting public dollars to private schools—that is, as a political effort "to reform public education out of existence through a strategy of 'test and burn'" (Karp, 2003, p. 4). Gerald Bracey calls the law "a weapon of mass destruction" with the public schools as its target (quoted in Karp, 2003, p. 4).

PROVISIONS OF THE NO CHILD LEFT BEHIND ACT

The No Child Left Behind Act recasts and expands the federal role in public schooling, especially for schools that receive funding through Title I of ESEA, the primary federal aid program for schools in high-poverty areas. Through its provisions, backed by sanctions for noncompliance, the sweeping law covers these areas of school practice, among others:

- Testing. The law requires schools to test all children in Grades 3 through 8 every year and specifies increasingly severe consequences for schools that do not show steady progress toward a goal of 100% student proficiency on state assessments. By the 2005–2006 school year, states must begin testing students in reading and math, using assessments aligned with state academic standards. By 2013–2014, states must show that *all* students, including those with disabilities and those learning English, are scoring in the proficient range.

  Before then, schools must make steady progress toward this goal, based on a formula spelled out in the law, both for the student body as a whole and for subgroups, including racial and ethnic minorities and students from low-income families as well as students with disabilities and students with limited fluency in English. Schools that fail to meet annual performance targets, and so to make "adequate yearly progress," for 2 years in a row are tagged "in need of improvement." Schools receiving Title I money that miss the targets for 2 years in a row must allow students to transfer to other public schools. Districts must pay for students' transportation to other schools, and some funding shifts from the "failing" schools to the new schools. A school that fails to make adequate progress for a third year must also pay for private tutoring and other services, such as before- or after-school programs in reading, language arts, and math. Neither schools "in need of improvement" nor districts deemed "failing" can provide these services to their own students (Miner, 2003, p. 5). If a school continues to make inadequate progress, more drastic measures loom, such as hiring a new principal and staff or closing the school and reopening it as a charter school.

- Public reporting. Since 2002–2003, states have been required to publish annual report cards showing student achievement data, including subgroup breakdowns, as well as information on the performance of school districts. Districts must make similar public reports with school-level data.
- Teacher competence. By the end of the 2005–2006 year, public schools are to have a "highly qualified" teacher in every classroom. Starting in 2002–2003, all new teachers hired with Title I money were to have been "highly qualified," and by the end of the 2005–2006 year, paraprofessionals hired with this money are to have completed at least 2 years of college, obtained an associate's degree, or passed an evaluation to demonstrate knowledge and teaching ability.
- Military recruiting. A provision in the law that has attracted much less attention than the testing and hiring mandates gives the Pentagon access to high school directories with students' names, addresses, and phone numbers. School districts receiving Title I funding must give military recruiters this information, unless students and parents formally object. Districts that do not comply risk losing the aid.

A CHORUS OF COMPLAINTS

An outcry of protests accompanied implementation of the No Child Left Behind Act. The *New York Times* reported "nearly universal contempt for this noble-sounding law" (Winerip, 2003a). The National Education

Association (NEA), the nation's largest teachers union, announced plans to challenge the law in a suit filed on behalf of states, school districts, and teachers. The law, which "poses as Dr. Jekyll but is really the evil Mr. Hyde," is turning out to be "the granddaddy of all underfunded federal mandates," said NEA president Reg Weaver (Keller, 2003b). Groups such as the Citizens' Commission on Civil Rights have expressed concern that the law will institutionalize a "dual" system of public schooling—one for schools receiving Title I money, which can be redirected, and another for other schools (Olson, 2003b).

Harvard education professor Richard Elmore has called the law "the single largest, and the single most damaging, expansion of federal power over the nation's education system in history" (quoted in Dillon, 2003a). Michigan Education Commissioner Tom Watkins characterized it as "a vehicle to bash our teachers and kids" and predicted that 85% of the schools in his state will be declared failing (Winerip, 2003a). The Children's Defense Fund (2001b), whose trademark mission has long been to "leave no child behind," warned that these words ought not "become a fig leaf for unjust political and policy choices that, in fact, will leave millions of children and the poor behind."

Rural school leaders pointed out that teachers in small high schools often teach multiple subjects: history, geography, and American government, for example, or biology, chemistry, and physics. Requiring these teachers to prove themselves "highly qualified" in every subject they teach, which generally means having a separate college degree in each subject, could force thousands of them either to go back to school or, more likely, to move to more populated areas where they can teach a single subject. Apart from the need to find and hire teachers with multiple certifications, rural schools struggle to compete with more generously funded urban and suburban districts to attract good teachers. The average teacher in a rural area makes only 86 cents for every dollar earned by his or her counterpart in urban and suburban schools. In 13 states, the pay gap is more than $5,000 a year (Tompkins, 2003). Tompkins (2003) predicts that under No Child Left Behind, hard-to-staff schools will become harder to staff, as teachers in schools "needing improvement" look to move to schools in prosperous communities that can afford to pay more. The real losers then will be the students left behind in sub-par schools without the financial wherewithal to attract good teachers.

The requirement that students in schools "needing improvement" be allowed to transfer elsewhere has drawn protests from rural and urban schools leaders alike. After visiting a school on remote St. Lawrence Island in Alaska, where enforcing this provision would require flying students 164 miles across the Bering Sea to another school, Secretary of Education Rod Paige reportedly acknowledged the problem (Dillon, 2003c). Urban schools face a similar challenge, albeit for different reasons. In many districts all the schools are already at capacity or overcrowded. A *Washington Post* cartoon (reprinted in *Rethinking Schools*, 2003, p. 3) shows a puzzled teacher with an encyclopedic attendance roster asking the horde of students in front of her, "Wait a minute, when did our class size reach 3,704,552?" "This was the only school that wasn't failing, so they transferred all of us here," a student responds.

Although No Child Left Behind gives families the right to take students, and the federal government the right to take money, out of struggling schools, it does not guarantee students any new places to go. Letters went out in the spring of 2003 to families of 228,000 children in New York City entitled to transfer out of "failing" schools. The year before, 6,400 students in such schools requested transfers, but only 1,507 received them because students were permitted to transfer only within their districts and the New York City Board of Education was obligated to approve only as many transfers as it had seats available (Herszenhorn, 2003). In 2003, transfers were available citywide, but, again, only to schools with empty seats—a "huge escape hatch," said Frederick Hess of the American Enterprise Institute (quoted in Schemo, 2002c).

While drafting the law, Congress discussed but rejected a proposal to require states to allow students to transfer across district lines if there are too few "good schools" in their home districts to accommodate them (Schemo, 2002c, p. A26). Consequently, rich districts do not have to open their doors to students from poor districts. That is the reason Judy Garcia's child in the fall of 2003 started traveling 90 minutes each way by public transportation from her home in the far northern Bronx to a middle school in far southern Manhattan, even though the Garcias live near the border of Westchester County, which has some of the wealthiest schools and smallest classes in the nation. Overwhelmed by transfer students they did not expect, teachers in the Manhattan middle school initially made do with too few chairs and braced for class sizes of up to 40 students (Winerip, 2003c). Because the greatest disparities are between school districts rather than between schools within a single district, students in struggling schools are unlikely to end up in significantly better schools unless they can transfer to other districts.

The promise of free tutoring for poor children in failing schools also has not materialized for thousands of children in New York City (Gross, 2003). A group of parents filed a class-action lawsuit claiming that children assigned to failing schools in New York City and Albany were denied the opportunity to transfer or to receive the supplemental services required by No Child Left Behind. A federal court judge in Manhattan dismissed the suit in 2003 with the argument that Congress never intended "to create individually enforceable rights" with the law and that the opportunity-to-transfer option might not be available to all students ("Court dismisses lawsuit," 2003).

Small schools with few students in each grade, often the case in rural schools, face multiple problems in trying to implement No Child Left Behind. Year-to-year changes in the student body can cause wild fluctuations in test scores that lead to unwarranted judgments about the school. Before the law was passed, Kane and Staiger (2001) showed that random variation accounts for 70% of the year-to-year change in test scores for grade levels or schools. A study in Massachusetts predicts that annual variations in test scores will be three to four times greater in schools with fewer than 100 students per grade than in schools with more than 150 students (Tompkins, 2003). Also, as Tompkins (2003), president of the Rural School and Community Trust, points out, the reporting requirements can set up students for public humiliation: "When small-town newspaper readers find out, for example, that five out of 18 4th graders scored below proficiency in reading, there will likely be open speculation about who the five kids are."

The funding provided for No Child Left Behind has roused the biggest outcry, however. Although federal spending on education increased after the law was passed, the administration subsequently backtracked significantly on promises made while negotiating its passage. The education budget for 2004, for example, was $6 billion short of the amount the administration had agreed to provide (Schemo, 2003a)—a "skinflint budget" that "doesn't provide the boost in funding that would be needed to dramatically increase the number of qualified teachers," *The New York Times* editorialized ("Education reform," 2003, p. A16). "The administration likes to talk about the soft bigotry of low expectations and how this law fights that. But what about the hard bigotry of high expectations without adequate resources?" wondered Paul Houston, executive director of the American Association of School Administrators (quoted in Fletcher, 2003, p. A1). "If money indicates priorities, the president believes No Child Left Behind is one sixty-seventh as important as cutting taxes," observed Ross Wiener, policy analyst at the Education Trust, a nonprofit organization that has backed the No Child Left Behind Act (quoted in Schemo, 2003a).

After reviewing projected costs of fulfilling the requirements of No Child Left Behind in 10 states, Mathis (2003) warned that ensuring that all children pass the mandated tests comes with a stunning price tag. In seven of the 10 states, base costs of schooling would have to increase more than 24%, and in six of the seven states, 30% to 46%.[1] Public spending on K–12 education was $422.7 billion in 2001–2002. A lowball estimate of the funding required to fulfill the mandates of No Child Left Behind is an extra 20% for the nation as a whole, or an increase of $84.5 billion. To offer a perspective: In 2003, the administration proposed increasing the Title I appropriation by $1 billion, from $11.3 billion to $12.3 billion. Given the shortfall, legislators in Hawaii, Louisiana, Minnesota, Nebraska, and Utah have produced bills proposing that their states opt out of the law and accept a loss of federal aid to poor schools if necessary (Keller, 2003b).

Many states, wracked by mammoth budget crises, are leaving schools to fend for themselves in the face of the underfunded test-score mandates. Eisenhower Elementary in Oklahoma City is a case in point. At the end of the 2002–2003 school year, 600 teachers in Oklahoma City lost their jobs and seven schools were closed. More than half the city's 70 elementary schools failed to make adequate progress under the requirements of the federal law and 11 schools were deeming failing. Among them was Eisenhower. Although the school, which serves many low-income students, received federal funding for tutoring and other supports designed to raise test scores, the city sent layoff notices to half the school's teachers days before standardized tests were given. Not surprisingly, student performance fell short of Principal Angela Houston's hopes. "The teachers tried," she said, "but when you've just been told you don't have a job, it plays on your psyche." "It's hard for us now just to keep the grass mowed and the floors shined at our schools," said district superintendent Bob Moore (Dillon, 2003e, p. A28).

A U.S. General Accounting Office (2003b) extrapolation of testing-related costs alone in seven states found the federal funding allocated will cover the cost of developing and administering the tests required by No Child Left Behind. This is true, however, *only if states*

---

[1]Mathis (2003) looked at cost projections in Indiana, Maryland, Montana, Nebraska, New Hampshire, New York, South Carolina, Texas, Vermont, and Wisconsin.

use only multiple-choice tests easily scorable by machine. Funding is not adequate if states use their current assessments and falls grossly short if states opt to use new essay or open-ended questions.

Not surprisingly, military recruiters' new access to underage students also has raised questions. People like Glen Price, a school board member in Contra Costa County, California, question "the educational link between military recruiting and the goals and objectives of No Children Left Behind" (quoted in Lewin, 2003, p. B10). In fact, the Pentagon had been seeking access to high school students for years and regards No Child Left Behind as an important tool in meeting its goal of attracting 210,000 young people each year to full-time military service, and another 150,000 to the Reserves or National Guard (Lewin, 2003, p. B10). In testimony before a government commission, Marine Corps Master Sergeant John Bailey explained the challenge: "Our war starts at the school .... Counselors would rather sell college" (quoted in Jordan, 2003, p. 9).

FEARS OF LARGE-SCALE FAILURES

A number of estimates have been put forth about how many schools are at risk of failing under No Child Left Behind. "The Center for Assessment says 75%, North Carolina estimates 60%, Vermont calculated 80% over three years, and Louisiana reports 85%—even though two-thirds of their schools show improved scores" (Mathis, 2003). In the summer of 2002, more than 8,000 high-poverty schools were deemed failing (Schemo, 2003a). Of the 227 schools in Ohio with at least 30 African-American students, more than 90% would have failed to make adequate progress in 2001–2002 based on that subgroup's test scores (Olson, 2003a). "I don't know of any state that isn't facing pretty staggering numbers" in terms of schools not meeting the law's requirements, said Michael Ward, president of the Council of Chief State School Officers (quoted in Fletcher, 2003, p. A1). Reports in August 2003 showed that 3,200 of the 7,100 schools in California subject to the federal law failed to make adequate progress and 1,135 "needed improvement," 2,500 of Florida's 3,000 schools failed to make adequate progress and 48 were rated as needing improvement, and 1,250 of Pennsylvania's 2,800 schools failed to make adequate progress while 171 were tagged as needing improvement (Dillon, 2003e).

Schools with diverse populations—which is to say many high-poverty schools—are particularly at risk. With far more subgroups than many other schools, these schools have many more "opportunities" to fail to meet yearly targets. "A failing label will be assigned frequently, based on the crushing impact of poverty," Lowell Russell (cited in Mathis, 2003) warned in an analysis prepared for the Indiana Urban Superintendents Association. The August 2003 report showed that 365 of Chicago's 600 schools needed improvement, which means students in these schools must be allowed to transfer. To where is a good question. Approximately 240,000 parents subsequently were told they could compete for about 1,000 seats for their children at better-performing schools.

Not surprisingly, "creative approaches" to the mandates of No Child Left Behind were evident in the early years of implementation. Although the law requires adequate yearly progress toward the goal of 100% proficiency, states have considerable leeway in determining what counts as success. Fearful of the sanctions the law prescribes, many states lowered their own standards to decrease the risk of failure. Texas, for example, reduced the number of questions students must answer correctly to pass the third-grade reading test. Colorado overhauled its grading system so that scores previously in the "partially proficient" category now fall in the "proficient" category. Michigan lowered its initial starting point for the percentage of high school students who must pass the English test for a school to show adequate progress from 75% to 42%, and thereby reduced the number of schools needing improvement from 1,513 to 216 (Dillon, 2003a). The remaining 216 schools overwhelmingly are in poor communities—96 in Detroit, 18 in Flint, and 15 in Grand Rapids (Keller, 2003a). Many states also planned, and gained federal approval for, back loading achievement with steep gains in the final years. Ohio, for example, vowed to raise the percentage of students who pass statewide tests from 40% to 60% in 6 years, an average gain of 3.3 percentage points each year, but then, starting in 2010, to raise the percentage to 100% in just 4 years, an average gain of 10 percentage points a year (Dillon, 2003a).

North Carolina, which opted not to change its 10-year-old school accountability system, has ended up in the preposterous position of having schools that are both "excellent" and at risk of failing. At the end of the 2002–2003 school year, half the schools in the state were cited for failing to make adequate progress under the federal law. Yet hundreds of these same schools were eligible for bonuses from the state, based on the state's own assessment, which rewards schools with high numbers of proficient students as well as schools that start far behind but show significant progress.

One such school is T.C. Berrien Elementary in Fayetteville. School Principal Jacqueline McLeod took on the job with fervor. She attracted some outstanding teachers to the school, used state funds to reduce class sizes and to offer a mentoring program, helped raise $50,000 for a playground, and cancelled a 3-week fall break in the school's year-round schedule when she thought the children needed the time in school. "That Monday, just 50 showed up," she recalled. "I told the bus drivers, 'Find the rest.' We spent the morning calling homes. By Thursday I had them all" (quoted in Winerip, 2003b, p. B7). All the hard work paid off. By the end of the year, 66% of the students, 90% of whom receive free lunches and 99.9% of whom are African-American, were at a proficiency level in reading and math on the state tests. The state cited Berrien as a high growth school in June 2003 and gave teachers $1,500 bonuses. A few weeks later, the federal assessment system showed the school barely missed its yearly target. Because this was the second year in a row, Berrien was sanctioned. "It didn't reflect the work we did last year," a disappointed McLeod said of the federal sanctions. "I can show you how far I brought [the children]. They grew" (quoted in Winerip, 2003b, p. B7).

FIXING THE WRONG PROBLEM

Sadly, No Child Left Behind appears, at best, to fix the wrong problem. The sanctions written into the law seem designed to compel teachers to teach and students to learn. Yet, few children do not want to learn and few teachers do not want to teach. This is hardly the biggest problem in struggling schools. What is missing is opportunity and support, not desire. Consider the gap between the reforms institutionalized through No Child Left Behind and the needs of John Essex, a high-poverty school in rural Demopolis, Alabama. *The New York Times* (Schemo, 2002b), reported:

> The truck full of stones showed up at John Essex School without explanation, as if some unnamed saint had heard Loretta McCoy's despair. As principal of this school in Alabama's rural Black Belt, Ms. McCoy struggles to find money for essentials: library books, musical instruments, supplies and teachers. So when the stones appeared, Ms. McCoy knew it might be the closest John Essex would get to landscaping and got pushing.
>
> A pile went by the back door, filing a huge pothole the children waded through when it rained. Another truckload filled a sinkhole by the Dump-

> sters, where garbage trucks got stuck in mud, and a third went to craters when the children took recess. Her pleading got John Essex five deliveries of rock: not enough to level the school's entrance, but enough to give its principal a small dose of hope.

The K–12 school has 264 students, all poor and all Black. The building's cinder-block walls are unplastered, electrical lines are exposed, and the library includes books "that ponder how the Vietnam War will turn out" and "speak of landing on the moon as an ambitious dream" (Schemo, 2002b). Students must master a foreign language to earn the academic diploma they need to get into college, but the school has no foreign language teacher, also no art or music teacher. A few wrist bells constitute the school's collection of musical instruments. One person teaches chemistry, earth science, biology, and all the other science classes.

Given the funding shortfalls and high failure rates widely predicted for struggling schools like John Essex, it is hard to believe that sanctions are a good-faith prescription for success. Schools with fewer students and less funding will have even more difficulty attracting the best teachers, most of whom will choose not to teach in a school branded "failing." Although No Child Left Behind was signed into law with promises of "not giving up on a single student," which suggests a commitment to ensuring that all children succeed, sanctions drive the law and almost ensure the opposite: failure. If this was not the case, if a state documented the success of each and every student, that state no doubt "would be castigated for cheating, grade inflation, or low standards" (Gratz, 2003). "Pious platitudes about children being able to learn and accountability for adequate yearly progress" are poor substitutes for "the cold, hard cash" (Tompkins, 2003) schools like John Essex need to attract good teachers and to fund the programs that might substantiate this rhetoric.

Although the federal contribution to total spending on public education is very small, about 7%, the high-poverty schools most vulnerable to the sanctions rely disproportionately on this money (Schemo, 2003a). No Child Left Behind appears not to address the very real problems in these schools, some of which rely on Title I dollars for more than a third of their spending ("Threat," 1999), but rather to use those problems as a rationale for eroding public education.

President Bush wanted to include vouchers for private schools in the No Child Left Behind law, but let this go when it became clear Congress would not pass the legislation with that provision. Arguably, however, No Child Left Behind lays the groundwork for exactly this outcome. The goal seems to be not to improve the quality of schooling for poor children, but rather "to turn the problems of poor schools into a campaign to destroy public education" (Karp, 2003, p. 4). As more and more schools are deemed failing, the demand for vouchers likely will increase, paving the way for a transfer of students and funds to private schools.

In the summer of 2003, the president revived his call for vouchers and backed a proposal to spend $75 million in federal money on vouchers for private schools. Of the $75 million, $15 million would go to families in Washington, DC for vouchers for 2,000 of the 67,000 students in the district. The move came after a decision by the U.S. Supreme Court the year before that affirmed the constitutionality of allowing parents to use public funds to pay for religious and other private schooling. The case focused on a program in Cleveland, which provides private-school vouchers of up to $2,250 to approximately 3,700 of the district's 75,000 students.

Many students lack supports common in middle-class and affluent households—an adult at home in the evening, lots of books, a quiet place to work. Others struggle to cope with the stress of living with chronic economic insecurity—evictions, homelessness, moving from place to place—or of living in a community used by the larger society as a toxic dumping ground. By ignoring this reality, No Child Left Behind continues the "blame-the-victim approach" that has long characterized public schooling. Much more is required than simply proclaiming we now have high expectations for all children. Unaccompanied by a political commitment "to build a system where there is a reason to expect every child to succeed" (Gratz, 2003), such proclamations mock the ideals they evoke.

Under the guise of battling "the soft bigotry of low expectations," policy-makers are moving in the wrong direction in the long struggle to realize the ideal of equal educational opportunity. The stick side of the No Child Left Behind Act is operating: Schools unable to meet annual achievement targets are being punished. However, the carrot side of the law, something better for poor children in struggling schools, has not materialized. Although funding for Title I has increased,[2] it falls wildly short of the realistic costs of achieving "100% proficiency."

---

[2]The formula for distributing Title I dollars itself creates educationally unjustifiable disparities. Among New York City boroughs, for example, Staten Island, with moderate levels of poverty, receives much less funding through Title I than the Bronx, with stunning levels of poverty. However, because relatively few schools on Staten Island have significant concentrations of poverty, the dollars are split very few ways. The relatively large Title I allocation to the Bronx, where nine out of every ten schools exceed the poverty threshold, must be divided up among many more schools. Consequently, students in Title I schools on Staten Island end up with almost three times as much in funding as students in schools in the Bronx. Because the No Child Left Behind Act leaves the funding formula intact, increases in Title I funding likely will exacerbate the existing disparities among New York City boroughs, which in 2002 were as large as $1,431 per child (Winter, 2002).

HEAD START

As the federal government reviewed states' plans for implementing No Child Left Behind in summer 2003, a related battle gathered steam when the Bush administration proposed to overhaul Head Start, the federally funded preschool program that serves almost 1 million of the nation's poorest 3- and 4-year-olds in community centers and schools. Under the proposal, the funding for the program would be distributed in block grants to states, under the control initially of up to eight governors. When Head Start was created in 1965 as an initiative within the larger War on Poverty, then-President Lyndon Johnson deliberately avoided giving governors, antagonists in battles over civil rights, control over the program (Bumiller, 2003).

Critics of the proposal, including more than 40 antipoverty and child welfare groups, protested that distributing Head Start dollars in block grants to states would dismantle the program by destroying the federal guarantee that the money will be used as originally intended—namely, to provide an array of services to poor children, including nutritional food, dental and health care, immunizations, and, in some centers, literacy programs for family members. "To take this program away from communities—this is a direct federal community program—[and] hand it over to states without the national performance standards, without the requirements for comprehensive services that make Head Start successful, and at a time when states are facing the biggest budget deficits in their history, is to destroy it," said Marion Wright Edelman, founder and president of the Children's Defense Fund (Smiley, 2003).

Under the proposal, Head Start employees would be required to teach reading, writing, and math skills, and Head Start pupils would be required to participate in an assessment to determine if the new academic standards were being met. The proposal would require at least half of all Head Start teachers to have 4-year college degrees by 2008, but would not require competitive salaries. Head Start teachers now earn only about half the average salary of kindergarten teachers (Schemo, 2003a).

HIGH-STAKES TESTING, STANDARDS, AND ACCOUNTABILITY

No Child Left Behind and the proposal to revamp Head Start both drive and reflect a larger educational reform movement that attempts to hold schools accountable for raising standards through practices of high-stakes testing. Such practices have swept the nation, despite continuing and significant disparities in school funding (see chap. 6), despite state budget crises that threaten to exacerbate these disparities, despite the fact that almost every state constitution includes language that gives the state (not individual schools or school districts) final responsibility for public education, and despite a host of problems with the tests themselves. The testing industry's own code of conduct specifies that standardized tests should not be used to make life-altering decisions about students. A host of organizations, including the American Educational Research Association, the nation's largest educational research group, have publicly opposed the practice of using a single test to make a high-stakes decision (Henriques & Steinberg, 2001, p. A1).

A large national study challenges fundamental assumptions about the relationship between high-stakes testing and student learning. Amrein and Berliner (2002b) looked at academic achievement in the 27 states with the highest stakes written into their Grades 1–8 testing policies and in the 18 states with make-or-break exams for high school graduation. The review led them to conclude that high-stakes testing not only fails to foster student learning, but sometimes even reduces it:

> After the implementation of high-stakes tests, nothing much happens. That is, no consistent effects across states were noted, scores seem to go up or down in a random pattern, after high-stakes tests are introduced .... [Also] after the implementation of high school graduation exams, academic achievement apparently decreases .... On balance, these analyses suggest that high-stakes tests and high school graduation exams may tend to inhibit the academic achievement of students, not foster their academic growth. (Amrein & Berliner, 2002b, pp. 57–58)

Using National Assessment of Educational Progress scores as a measure of student learning, the researchers found that after high stakes were attached to tests, eighth-grade math achievement increased slightly. However, fourth-grade math achievement decreased, and fourth-grade reading achievement stayed about the same overall. After states implemented high school graduation exams, scores on the ACT, the Scholastic Aptitude Test, and Advanced Placement exams declined overall.

Faced with the prospect of denying diplomas to tens of thousands of students, states have thrown out test results or postponed consequences of high-stakes exams. In New York, the state's education commissioner threw out scores on the 2003 Regents math exams for juniors and seniors, a requirement for graduation, after the Council of School Superintendents estimated that 70% of the test takers had failed. Scores for ninth and tenth graders subsequently were raised so that thousands of students who initially failed the Math A Regents exam ended up passing it (Arenson, 2003b). The year before, 39% of the students (among the smartest in the state) who took the Regents physics exam failed it—a failure rate more than double that on tests given in 2000 and 2001 (Dillon, 2003d). Georgia earlier pushed back its "end of course" exam for a year, and Alaska delayed its high school exit exam, originally planned for 2002, for 2 years. Just after the uproar in New York, a state-sponsored study in California showed as many as 92,000 seniors, about one in every five, would fail the high school exit exam. The state Board of Education then decided to postpone the consequences of the exam for 2 years, until 2006. Advocates for poor and minority students argued that the delay in and of itself will not alter the disparate impact the exam likely will have on these students because it does not address the lack of qualified teachers and successful schools in poor neighborhoods (Winter, 2003).

Then there is the matter of test scoring. *The New York Times* reported in 2001 that millions of students in at least 20 states had been affected by errors in scoring standardized proficiency tests, and concluded, "The [testing] industry cannot guarantee the kind of error-free, high-speed testing that parents, educators, and politicians seem to take for granted" (Henriques & Steinberg, 2001, p. A1). In the prior 3 years, NCS Pearson, the nation's largest test scorer, produced a flawed answer key that lowered multiple-choice scores for 12,000 Arizona students, made mistakes in adding up Michigan students' scores on essay tests, and was forced with another company to rescore 204,000 essay tests in Washington because the state thought the scores should be lower. An error by another big company, CTB/McGraw-Hill, resulted in almost 9,000 students in New York City being mistakenly assigned to summer school in 1999. A *New York Times* investigation found that testing officials in New York City, Indiana, and other school districts had repeatedly warned CTB that percentile scores seemed wrong, but the company told each not to worry, while declining to mention the other complaints. Then, after finding a critical programming error, CTB officials waited 7 weeks before telling the school districts about the problem. The testing industry has fended off several proposals for federal oversight. Consequently, companies themselves decide what they will disclose and when (Steinberg & Henriques, 2001, p. A1).

Practices of high-stakes testing take a particularly harsh toll on poor students and students of color who are failing make-or-break exams in disproportionate numbers, undoubtedly because they are being tested on material they have not been taught or been taught well (Amrein & Berliner, 2002a; Livingston & Livingston, 2002). Many, it seems, are opting to drop out of school rather than face tests they suspect they cannot pass (Amrein & Berliner 2002a), often with the encouragement of administrators seeking to exclude low scores from their schools' tallies (McNeil, 2000; Orel, 2003; Schemo, 2003b). Dropout rates among English language learners in New York City increased sharply—to the point where more of these students were dropping out than were graduating—after 1999 when New York made a passing score on the English Language Arts Regents exam, which presumes a native fluency, a requirement for graduation (New York Immigration Coalition and Advocates for Children, 2002).

A state audit in Houston schools showed test scores rose as the number of test takers declined along with the district's publicly reported dropout rate. The audit confirmed what anecdotal evidence had already suggested: Eager to raise scores, some schools are pushing out "undesirable" students, then reporting dropout rates that hide the practice. The audit found that more than half the 5,500 students who left Houston schools in the 2000–2001 year should have been, but were not, counted as dropouts. Partly on the basis of the low dropout rate it reported of 1.5%, the district won a $1 million prize as the best urban district in the country. "It was Enron accounting," said a former employee of the district's office of research and accountability (Schemo, 2003b, p. A1). In one third of Houston's 30 high schools, standardized test scores went up while enrollment dropped. At Austin High, for example, 65% of the 2,757 students enrolled in 1998 passed the 10th-grade math test. Three years later, 99% of the 2,215 students enrolled passed the test. The school also reported a 92% decline in the dropout rate during this period, from 4.1% to 0.3%. "You're driving kids out who will skew your scores," said state representative Rick Noriega (Schemo, 2003b, p. A1).

The Houston schools are hardly the only ones that have been manipulating numbers. *The New York Times* (Lewin & Medina, 2003) reported a massive undercounting of dropouts in New York City as well. During the 2000–2001 school year, city schools "discharged" more than 55,000 high school students while graduating fewer than 34,000, and reported an official dropout rate of around 20%. The catch-all category of "discharged" includes students who move, transfer to private schools, and drop out of their own accord as well as students who are pushed out, presumably into "another educational setting." However, because many schools' record keeping is shoddy, at best, students are simply lost. When pressured to leave, many students do. Often, it seems, no one then knows, or seemingly cares, what becomes of them.

From one perspective, the fact that some students are not graduating proves the strength of the standards. If everyone could reach them, how high would they be? The judge in a high-profile case focused on high-stakes testing in Texas spoke for many when he argued that "receipt of an education that does not meet some minimal standards is an adverse impact just as surely as failure to receive a diploma" (*GI Forum v. TEA*, 2000, p. 13). From this perspective, the failures prove the success of the policy: Standards have been established and upheld.

Yet, the means to this end of upholding standards is the production of failure, using young people as the instruments of that production. In a study of newly legislated policies in Georgia designed to end "social promotion," Livingston and Livingston (2002) predicted that one third to one half of all fourth, sixth, and eighth graders in the 39 poorest counties in rural Georgia, a quarter of which fall into the "all-Black" school system category, will be held back. This practice almost certainly will increase dropout rates, albeit at a significant cost saving to the state. Livingston and Livingston (2002) raise the question pointedly:

> Is this legislation really intended to improve education or is it a strategy to reduce the State's financial obligation to the rural poor? It is clear that failing masses of poor children will not improve pedagogy because punishing children with retention does not change teaching. What we do know is that the association between retention and dropping out is noted consistently throughout educational research .... Because these 39 counties are very poor, and the tax base available for public schools is small, the State of Georgia compensates for this revenue deficiency by making exceptionally large contributions to these counties. Thus, while not stated as policy, it cannot be ignored that the CRCT [Criterion Referenced Competency Test Results] will most likely save the State a considerable amount of money by reducing the number of students in school in these counties.

Similar questions could be raised about the willingness of many other states to pay for the schooling of poor children, especially when squeezed by budget shortfalls.

From one perspective, the public reporting of test scores required by No Child Left Behind sheds needed light on the plight of the poorest districts (Koch, 1999). The law will give taxpayers "an X-ray of neglect," said Jim Watts of the Southern Regional Education Board, which advises states on education policy (quoted in Schemo, 2002b). "States have unwittingly backed themselves into an interesting position" by establishing standards all students are required to meet, as they now have "a moral and financial and legal obligation" to make sure all students do in fact have the opportunity to meet the standards, observed Hugh Price, president of the National Urban League (quoted in Koch, 1999). Early in 2004, approximately 18 states faced legal challenges to their school funding systems, fueled in part by information collected to comply with the requirements of No Child Left Behind (American Association of Colleges for Teacher Education, 2004). In what observers believed might be the first of many such suits, the Reading School District in December 2003 sued the Pennsylvania Department of Education over the law's requirements. Charging that Pennsylvania had failed to provide adequate technical and financial assistance, the district filed the suit after Pennsylvania cited 13 of the district's elementary, middle, and high schools for not meeting standards (Chute, 2003). At the same time, recent decisions in school funding cases (see chap. 6) suggest courts are not necessarily holding states to this higher standard of accountability and instead are allowing some to retreat from historic responsibilities.

Schooling has become almost the only path to a job that pays a living wage, and such jobs, in turn, almost the only path to social respect and any measure of economic security. Young people who do not graduate high school for the most part "lack basic job skills as well as solid literacy and numbers proficiencies, and they are neither working nor looking for jobs. They are not in vocational training. They are not in manufacturing. They are not part of the information age. They are not included in the American conversation" (Jack Wuest, quoted in Herbert, 2001). Given these social stakes, state accountability to students—versus school accountability to taxpayers—becomes critical.

The failure of No Child Left Behind and the broader standards and accountability movement to offer much to poor children could be regarded, most charitably, as a case of unintended and unforeseen consequences. More realistically, I believe, this wave of educational reform is unfolding, if not exactly as planned, nevertheless in ways that policymakers find tolerable. Caught between federal mandates and their own budget crises, some states, with the Bush administration's blessing, are scaling back commitments to public education in ways that are particularly damaging for poor children. States are failing to fulfill the No Child Left Behind requirements to staff every classroom with a "highly qualified" teacher and to provide meaningful alternatives to students in struggling schools, but are succeeding, at least in some cases, in finding ways to reduce their obligation to poor districts that rely heavily on state aid.

As the standards and accountability movement has grown, states across the nation have made promotion and graduation more difficult. At the same time, jobs paying a living wage have been all but closed to anyone without a high school diploma. With these higher stakes comes a greater responsibility for funding meaningful educational opportunity—funding in the broadest sense of supporting and making something possible. Although more money surely does not guarantee better schooling, demanding more of young people (and their teachers) without providing real opportunity is patently unfair.

Yet, even if courts nationwide required states to fund meaningful educational opportunity in all its complexity, what of the young people who still could not or would not jump through the hoops of accountability? In his critique of the assumptions underlying the public debate on standards, testing, and accountability, Proefriedt (2001) tells this story, from a biography of Lyndon Johnson:

> When he was a very young boy living on a farm with his parents, his closest playmate was a Mexican-American boy named Huisso. Young Lyndon wanted to race on horseback with Huisso. But Huisso's horse was thin and weak. Johnson took feed from his own bins and doubled the intake of Huisso's horse in an effort to make him stronger for the race. Twice they raced, and Johnson's horse won easily. "So we tried one more time," the young Lyndon said, "and Huisso pushed his horse hard as he had ever pushed anything. This time the horse seemed to be moving much faster, but in the middle of the race it simply slipped out from under him. It had collapsed. It was dead. It was too much, I guess, too much running, too much food, too much care. It just didn't seem fair after all we had done." (p. 50)

Proefriedt (2001) offers his own commentary:

> It's an un-American story. It breaks with the whole sense of future possibility that is so much a part of the American dream .... It's a dangerous story because it might be used by those who would turn back the clock on whatever efforts the nation is presently making for the educational opportunity of our poorest children. It is a troubling story, to me, because

> however much I want to believe in the infinite possibilities for every American child, I keep seeing that image of Huisso's dead horse. (p. 50)

I, too, am haunted by this prophetic image. Forced to compete in contests not made for them, many young people are paying the price for the widespread but generally unarticulated assumptions about human worth and potential that hover just beneath the surface of the standards and accountability movement. Our systems of school accountability gain moral legitimacy from the belief that anyone can make it, if he or she simply tries. The corollary, of course, is that anyone who does not lacks the requisite will power or strength of character. Such a belief comes at a cost: "Our sense of solidarity with our fellow citizens is lost by the wayside. We set our standards, assume some moral deficiency in those who cannot meet them, and consign them to a well-deserved poverty" (Proefriedt, 2001).

The standards and accountability movement has not reckoned with such fundamental moral questions as the relationship between those who set the standards of accountability and those who fail to meet them. Instead, it focuses narrowly on the relationship between schools and taxpayers and all too often takes as the measure of accountability the mere act of reporting out test scores. However, as Moran (2000) argues:

> High-stakes tests cannot work miracles in failing systems. The examinations are a yardstick and, yes, even a stick, but they are not a magic wand. And, unlike a television game show, America cannot conveniently arrange for those who fail the tests to disappear, nor can its responsibilities to these children be promptly forgotten.

The stakes have been raised for students, but supports for learning remain tied to highly inequitable and in many places wholly inadequate systems of funding. Addressing this problem will require a broad public consciousness of responsibility to young people, including and especially those harmed by systems of "accountability." In disproportionate numbers, the victims are poor children who tend to start school far behind their wealthier peers for a host of reasons and in this way are set up to fail before they even start school. However, whether then pushed out before test time to "protect" a school's scores or allowed to stay and used as evidence that the school is "not working," poor children lose while someone else gains—taxpayers, private providers of the supplemental services students are supposed to receive if their schools fail for 2 years in a row, those who would destroy public education altogether, or all of the above.

10

How Poverty Could Matter Less in Schooling

I know that education is the only valid passport from poverty.

—*Lyndon B. Johnson*[1]

With even the most enlightened leadership and all the best breaks, schools by themselves cannot dent the poverty, crime, and racial isolation that disfigure major American cities. In fact, unrealistic expectations for schools can retard the amelioration of social problems, as has happened throughout America's past, by obscuring the difficult redistributive issues that underlie them.

—*Katz (1995, p. 135)*

Poverty takes an enormous physical, emotional, and economic toll on families, neighborhoods, and communities and therefore on children and schools. Denying the significance of poverty in schooling in the face of decades of research, testimony, and common sense requires profound naïveté or a frightening level of willed ignorance. However, with a realistic agenda for educational reform grounded in a commitment to the educational well-being of all children, and a sincere pursuit of the historic social ideal of equal educational opportunity, poverty could matter far less. Such a pursuit would necessarily be part of a larger agenda of social reform to reduce poverty and the growing disparities between rich and poor and between the politically powerful and powerless.

Neither the No Child Left Behind Act nor the larger standards and accountability movement it reflects fit the bill. Linked to a

[1]Johnson made this remark in 1965 in Johnson City, Texas, upon signing the Elementary and Secondary Education Bill (*Public papers*, 1966).

misdiagnosis of the fundamental problem—"the soft bigotry of low expectations"—the law's unrealistic mandates have already left many children behind and promise to leave many more. Poor children suffer educationally not primarily because of "low expectations," but rather because they grow up in poverty and, when they get to school, get less than others. Poor children are more likely than others to suffer the anxiety that comes from ongoing exposure to violence; to be hungry or chronically tired; to endure untreated ear infections and tooth decay; to suffer the escalating consequences, including brain damage, of exposure to lead; and to live in families stressed to the breaking point by economic insecurity and the demands of low-wage, dead-end jobs. In school, poor children on the whole have fewer "highly qualified" teachers, fewer buildings in good repair conducive to learning, fewer extracurricular activities, fewer guidance counselors and nurses, school lunches that are less nutritious, and less of almost everything else that money can buy for schools.

Expectations arise from beliefs. We expect what we believe is likely to happen, and beliefs must be based on something more than loud assertions, such as those about the achievement targets all children and schools are now to meet (Gratz, 2003). It is unreasonable to believe either that the inequities documented in this book somehow do not matter or that schools can single-handedly reshape a class-stratified society that produces and tolerates enormous poverty. It is far more reasonable to conclude, with Anyon (1997) and many others, that the society shapes schools far more than the schools shape society, and that something better for poor children will require a serious effort to eradicate or at least reduce poverty:

> We are aware—and over 30 years of research has consistently demonstrated—that academic achievement in U.S. schools is closely correlated with student socioeconomic status. To really improve ghetto children's chances, then, in school and out, we must (in addition to pursuing school-based reform) increase their social and economic well-being and status before and while they are students. We must ultimately, therefore, eliminate poverty; we must eliminate the ghetto school by eliminating the underlying causes of ghettoization. (Anyon, 1997, p. 164)

Although public schools lack the power and the resources to eradicate poverty and ghettoization, they nevertheless have an important role to play in such a project. A realistic and advocacy-oriented agenda for educational reform could improve the school experience of poor children considerably while edging the society a step closer to its long-stated aspiration of providing equal educational opportunity.

A REALISTIC AGENDA

A school reform effort with promise for poor children would need to be realistic in terms of both funding and objectives. Unfortunately, the No Child Left Behind Act continues a long tradition of public promises to poor children unsubstantiated with adequate funding. O'Connor (2001) calls it "the Iron Law of Anti-Poverty Funding, under which no effort to help poor children, including public education, has ever been funded well or consistently enough to operate according to its original design." Head Start provides another example. Funding for the program has always fallen far short of the need and in 2003 served only 60% of eligible children (Schumacher & Mezey, 2003).

A promising school reform effort would need to be aligned with a realistic assessment of the limitations as well as the possibilities of public schooling. Historically, public schools have had neither adequate funding across the board nor an ambitious but realistic set of expectations (Katz, 1987, 1995). Although inadequacies and disparities have plagued public schools from the start, schooling historically has been put forth as the solution to a whole host of social challenges: immigration, industrialization, poverty, lack of economic opportunity, and, more recently, fears that the nation could lose its military and economic preeminence (National Commission on Excellence in Education, 1983).

The use of public schooling as a tool of federal social and economic policy can be traced back to the Great Society programs of the 1960s (Kantor & Lowe, 1995), if not to the origins of our system of public schooling (Katz, 1995). From the outset of the Great Society, "the idea that education could eliminate poverty and expand economic opportunity for racial minorities and the poor dominated thinking about social and economic policy" (Kantor & Lowe, 1995, p. 4). At the same time, this belief allowed the Kennedy and Johnson administrations to champion school reform as a solution to social and economic problems in lieu of more direct intervention in society and the labor market. Policymakers "turned to politically palatable proposals such as tax cuts to stimulate economic growth and job training and compensatory education programs that promised to do something for the poor without either antagonizing business by interfering in the labor market or alienating working- and middle-class voters by transferring income to the least advantaged" (Kantor & Lowe, 1995, p. 7). By the second half of the 1960s, education had become a centerpiece of social policy and its role in reducing poverty and disadvantage a matter of public debate (Silver & Silver, 1991, p. 3).

In many ways, this is understandable. As Traub (2000) notes sarcastically, "It's hard to think of a more satisfying solution to poverty than education. School reform involves relatively little money and no large-scale initiatives, asks practically nothing of the nonpoor and is accompanied by the ennobling sensation that comes from expressing faith in the capacity of the poor to overcome disadvantage by themselves" (p. 54). On the flip side, "The idea that schools by themselves can't cure poverty not only sounds like an un-American vote of no confidence in our capacity for self-transformation but also seems to flirt with ... racialist theories ... that educational inequality is rooted in biological inequality" (p. 54).

Even the strongest system of public schooling will not create jobs, support families, protect communities used as dumping grounds, shore up the social institutions (health care, public safety, etc.) on which all but the wealthiest depend, undo institutionalized racism, or safeguard the political foundations of a society that espouses democratic ideals even as stunning concentrations of power and wealth render the poor, the near-poor, and arguably the middle class politically powerless. Higher test scores will change none of this. At the same time, all of this hampers learning and restricts educational opportunity.

AN ADVOCACY-ORIENTED AGENDA

A promising school reform agenda must be grounded not only in realism, but also in commitment to the educational well-being of all children, understanding of the complexities involved in pursuing this social goal, and determination to follow through. In his study of "star teachers" of poor children, Haberman (1994) observed that these educators strive to understand, not judge. "As they interact with children and adults in schools their first thought is not to decide the goodness or badness of things but to understand events and communications. They are not moralistic. They don't believe that preaching is teaching" (p. 135). Educational policymaking needs the same orientation: less moralistic judgment and more understanding of the complexities involved in teaching and learning in a society misshapen by concentrations of poverty and wealth.

Addressing the problems we already know about would be a good place to start. For example, we already know overcrowded schools in central cities are breaking under the weight of concentrated poverty, diverse student needs, and funding grossly inadequate to respond meaningfully to those needs. We already know that schools in poor rural areas lack the funding to attract good teachers or to offer a broad educational program. And we know that helping nonnative speakers acquire an academic level of proficiency in English requires an investment of time, skill, and money that society has so far been unwilling to make. We do not need the massive testing mandated by the No Child Left Behind Act to show us the plight of poor children in schools. Indeed, much of the information in this book came from reading newspapers; it is not secret or even very hard to find.

We already know poor children benefit from the same things that help other children: good preschool programs, small classes, enough money for schools to buy the things they need. In a long-running, large-scale study of an intensive, federally funded preschool program in Chicago that offers education, family, and health services, Reynolds, Temple, Robertson, and Mann (2001) found that the poor and mostly Black children enrolled 15 years earlier in the program had higher graduation rates and completed more years of education than demographically similar children who did not participate. The researchers tracked 1,539 children from 1985 to 2000. In another study, a state-by-state analysis of National Assessment of Education Progress scores between 1990 and 1996, Grissmer, Flanagan, Williamson, and Kawata (2001) found a wide disparity in poor students' school performance. Not surprisingly, these students' achievement was highest in states with relatively high per-pupil spending, with relatively small student–teacher ratios, and with more public prekindergarten classes.

In a review of mathematics teaching and learning in poor communities, a task force created by the National Council of Teachers of Mathematics (NCTM; 2003) affirmed, again, that math achievement is lower in poor than in affluent communities, that this happens in part because high-poverty schools "face many challenges that are tied to those conditions of poverty," and that what would help is providing poor children with what many others already have—an organized curriculum with significant mathematics, appropriate instructional materials, schools that offer teachers competitive salaries, a program of sustained professional development, and stable conditions conducive to teaching and learning. Haberman (1991) made essentially the same point in broader terms. Poor children do not need "the pedagogy of poverty" to which they are often subjected, he argued, but rather good teaching (p. 290). "If we but took the simple step of assuring that poor and minority children had teachers of the same quality as other children, about half of the achievement gap would disappear," The Education Trust (1998) similarly argued (p. 2).

More broadly, we already know that poor children suffer disproportionately in a whole host of ways that affect their social, emotional, physical, and cognitive development and hence their school performance. Citing a study that found poor children who got free breakfast at school showed significant test-scores gains compared with children who were eligible for the breakfast program but did not participate, Rothstein (2001) argues that addressing the problem of child hunger and deteriorating nutrition might be the most cost-effective educational reform measure the society could undertake:

> Iron deficiency anemia, which is twice as common in poor as in better-off children, affects cognitive ability. In experiments where pupils got inexpensive vitamin and mineral supplements, test scores rose from that treatment alone .... A higher minimum wage that helps low-wage parents feed their children could be one important step in ensuring that no child is left behind. And those wanting to narrow academic gaps can also take matters into their own hands, without relying on government: they can contribute to the nation's overstressed food banks. This too would amount to real education reform. (p. B8)

The relationship between poverty and education is complex. Many children who grow up in poverty excel academically—through hard work, their own giftedness, family support, dedication of teachers and other mentors, scholarships that enable them to pursue higher education, and so on. Poverty matters, but does not consign anyone to any fate. At the same time, it is tempting to point to inspirational stories of individual success and then jump to the opposite conclusion that poverty does not matter at all. That some young people succeed despite enormous social odds is a credit to them, never a reason to abdicate responsibility for creating the social conditions in which all children can flourish and in which no child pays the price for social priorities that devalue his or her health, safety, or educational well-being.

"NO EXCUSES": A FALSE MAP

With this temptation in mind, I want to offer a critique and invite thought about the politics involved in the popular rhetoric of "no excuses" in talk about education and poverty. *No Excuses*, a book published in 2000 as part of the Heritage Foundation's campaign by the same name, makes clear that its target is "the educational establishment and its apologists" (Carter, 2000, p. 2) who allegedly claim "that the legacies of poverty, racism, and broken families cannot be overcome when it comes to educating our nation's neediest" and consequently "that poor children are uneducable" (p. 7). A member of the "education establishment" myself, I know of no one who makes this claim. Nevertheless, in positioning itself against such alleged beliefs, proponents of "no excuses" encourage us to equate belief in the educability of all children with a particular school reform agenda, and to discount anyone who questions this agenda.

I saw the power of this rhetoric when I interviewed principals and assistant principals of high-poverty schools in upstate New York several years ago (Books, 2001). The school leaders spoke straightforwardly about what poverty means for their students—hunger, unstable housing, frequent moves, and so on—but also minimized the significance of all this in their work. "We don't want to be seen as making excuses," an assistant principal told me when I asked explicitly about her seeming reluctance to speak candidly.

A fear constrains public discussion of the educational significance of poverty and lends support to the idea that maybe poverty does not matter so much after all; it is just a matter of expectations. However, like the conspiracy of silence in the face of the nakedness of Hans Christian Andersen's vain emperor, silence about the significance of poverty in schooling serves other purposes. Although often touted as a way of providing hope and encouragement, discounting the significance of poverty simply saddles poor children and their families, teachers, and school leaders with the problems no longer publicly discussed.

Traub (2000) acknowledges the difficulty of arguing, as he nevertheless does, that "educational inequality is rooted in economic problems and social pathologies too deep to be overcome by school alone" and states as "painful" fact his belief that over the last 35 years "we have fiddled with practically everything you could think to fiddle with" in an effort to improve the opportunities of poor children, albeit with little result (p. 54). Arguably, "fiddle" is all we have done, with little conviction, inadequate funding, and so, predictably, little result. Nevertheless, Traub (2000) understands the politics of the discourse: "Why say anything [about the efficacy of schooling] that could discourage the children, parents and teachers who so desperately need encouragement?" (p. 54).

This is a false choice. It is not necessary to choose between (a) providing young people with the hope and encouragement they all need and (b) confronting the challenges of schooling in a stratified and highly diverse society ridden with poverty. "Encouragement" severed from understanding of the toll poverty takes on children merely sets the stage for exporting blame—to poor children and families, to teachers and administrators, to teacher educators, or all of the above. Profession of faith, even blind faith, in public schooling as a stair-step to doors of opportunity is not the only alternative to the implied counterview of resignation and defeat. Recognizing the toll poverty takes on children does not require "making excuses" for low achievement while throwing up one's hands before a social structure regarded as unalterable. Unfortunately, a powerful public discourse encourages exactly this sort of polarized thinking.

Consider the popular film "Stand and Deliver," based on former high school teacher Jaime Escalante's work with Chicano students in a Los Angeles barrio. Early in the film the school principal shares some bad news with his math faculty: The school will lose accreditation unless student achievement improves by the end of the year. The school, Garfield High, is depicted as an awful place: The principal calls the students "little bastards," students strip teachers' cars, a physical education instructor doubles as a math teacher, and parents seemingly care little about their children's education. "If we fail, we'll be put on probation," the principal warns. Offended, the chair of the math department protests: "If *we* fail? You can't teach logarithms to illiterates. These kids come to us with barely a seventh-grade education. If you want higher test scores, start by changing the economic level of the community. There isn't a teacher here who isn't doing everything he possibly can." At this critical juncture Escalante speaks up:

"I'm not. I could teach more."

"What do you need?" the principal asks, skeptical but intrigued.

"*Ganas*," Escalante replies. "That's all I need is *ganas*."

As the story unfolds, Escalante seemingly proves his point that given adequate desire and perseverance on the part of teacher and students alike, the effects of poverty, years of low-quality schooling, and institutionalized racism can be overcome. Escalante invites those unwilling to play by his rules to free up their seats. Some do, but those who stay end up passing the Advanced Placement (AP) calculus exam with flying colors—twice, the second time to disprove disbelievers at the Educational Testing Service. We learn at the end of the film that this level of achievement was not a fluke. For at least 5 years thereafter, the number of Garfield students passing the AP calculus exam continued to rise.

One cannot help but cheer for these students and their teacher who work so hard and deserve every bit of the public recognition they finally receive for their considerable accomplishments. Escalante seems to find a long-sought sense of meaning and purpose in his life, and the students grow in confidence and competence. Racism is outed, individual potential affirmed, and the skeptical department chair seems clearly proved wrong.

Yet the film offers a false map of the problem in juxtaposing Escalante's belief that, given the requisite desire, schooling can open doors of opportunity and render social injustices irrelevant, and his department chair's suggestion that trying do to this is an exercise in futility. Thinking about schooling and poverty need not be framed in this polarized way. A long tradition of scholarship supports the view, caricatured in the film, that for the most part schools reflect and shore up broader societal structures and therefore do little to "level the playing field." Sadly, the plethora of test scores now showing up in newspapers across the nation does little to challenge this thoroughly documented observation. The numbers say nothing at all, of course, about individual students' potential to learn, but speak volumes about the school experience of poor children—that is, about what poverty actually means in schooling.

I stress this point not to argue for resignation, but rather to critique the conceptual straitjacket perpetrated in films like "Stand and Deliver," in talk about tolerating "no excuses," and in federal laws like No Child Left Behind purportedly aimed at "low expectations." The suggestion that schools can do either everything or nothing is a pseudo choice, a stacked deck. Who's going to side with the naysayers? Mapping the conceptual terrain in this way—two choices, only one of which is morally tenable—seriously constrains informed discussion of the significance of poverty in schooling. When hopelessness and fatalism become the only imaginable alternative to blind faith in schooling, the latter wins out and get-tough policies that "hold schools accountable" for social injustices seem to make sense.

"INEQUALITY AT THE STARTING GATE"

Undoing the injustices that have created the disparities that leave poor children perpetually on the short end of the stick (with nowhere near enough Jaime Escalantes to go around) requires far more than an absence of low expectations or of "excuses." By the time poor children start school, they are already behind others for a whole host of reasons that are largely environmental in nature. "Disadvantaged children start kindergarten with significantly lower cognitive skills than their more advantaged counterparts. These same disadvantaged children are then placed in low-resource schools, magnifying the initial inequality" (Lee & Burkam, 2002, p. 1). An analysis of the U.S. Department of Education's Early Childhood Longitudinal Study (Lee & Burkam, 2002) showed that the average cognitive score of children in the highest of five socioeconomic groups was 60% above the score of children in the lowest group. Of the many factors the researchers considered—including race/ethnicity, family educational expectations, and access to quality child care—socioeconomic status accounted for more of the variation in cognitive scores than any other by far.

Given this "inequality at the starting gate" (Lee & Burkam, 2002), reducing achievement gaps between rich and poor children will require devoting considerable time, attention, and funding to students who come to school already "behind." Eliminating disparities in funding, qualified teachers, class sizes, safe buildings, and so on, would help, but this is a first step only—and a step likely, at best, to minimize the extent to which schooling magnifies other social inequalities. As Rothstein (2000) argues, "Using schools to combat social rigidities requires a lot of compensatory work for the less advantaged. Offering the same academic instruction to all will not work .... [I]f all children cannot get to an even starting gate, the race for rewards will continue to be a sham" (p. B13). Given a history of discrimination and disadvantage, simply stopping the practices does not level the playing field.

As we have seen, courts have not required states and districts to address this problem. The landmark *Brown v. Board of Education* decision by the U.S. Supreme Court in 1954 overturned the *Plessy* doctrine of separate-but-equal for schools segregated by race and by law, but did not require the provision of equal opportunity in a broader arena. Almost 20 years later, the U.S. Supreme Court recognized stark disparities in school funding among rich and poor districts in Texas, but found that poor children—more specifically, children of low-income families in property-poor districts—were not a "suspect class" (*San Antonio v. Rodriguez*, 1973). An alternate finding would have raised the bar for the state and made it more difficult to justify a school funding scheme that left poor children with so little compared to others.

In 1996, in a ruling that seemed promising to some advocates for poor children (Century Foundation, 2000; McUsic, 1999), the Connecticut Supreme Court found that the racial isolation of children in the Hartford public schools violated the state's constitution and was the primary factor contributing to the poor performance of the students in these high-poverty schools. The court in *Sheff v. O'Neill* declined to specify a remedy, and a political struggle to address the problem continued at least through 2003 when lawmakers approved a plan to open eight new magnet schools in the Hartford area to try to reduce racial isolation (Archer, 2003). Nevertheless, the remedy plaintiffs initially sought—redrawing school district lines to eliminate high-poverty districts—resonated with others. After the wave of court rulings in the 1990s that dismantled the desegregation directives fueled by *Brown* (Orfield, 1996), several districts tried to improve student performance by integrating schools on the basis of income rather than race.

LaCrosse, Wisconsin, was the first district to endorse economic integration when it did so in 1993. Test scores since then have gone up, despite a poverty rate that is still relatively high (Rimer, 2003). The Cambridge school district adopted a policy in 2002 designed to reduce sharp differences among schools in the percentage of students qualifying for subsidized meals, which in 2002 ranged from 21% in some schools to 72% in others. The policy has its critics. "There's something wrong with the assumption that if you've got too many low-income kids in a classroom, you can't teach them," said Abigail Thernstrom, a senior fellow at the Manhattan Institute. "My response to that is: No excuses. Start to educate the kids .... What are you going to do—helicopter the kids in?" (quoted in Rimer, 2003). In fact, the 6.2-square-mile Cambridge district is so small that no one needs to travel very far.

The Wake County district in North Carolina, which includes Raleigh, decided in 2000 to factor family income into student assignments, starting in 2002, to try to limit the number of students receiving subsidized lunches to no more than 40% at any school. There, too, the plan has faltered in the face of protest by suburban parents, despite the fact that the district's schools have been doing well (using state test scores as a gauge) and that long bus rides have fallen most heavily on the poorest students. Parents have complained that the school-assignment plan "trumps their ability to decide where their children should attend school" and is "unfair after they bought homes near the area's most reputable schools" (Richard, 2002, p. 1). After parents from the town of Apex organized, protested at school board meetings, and picketed the school district headquarters, their children were allowed to stay in neighborhood schools. "This is not easy," said the district superintendent. "It is very, very emotional in any community, but it is the right thing to do" (Richard, 2002, p. 19).

New York's highest court ruled in 2003 against the Rochester City School District in a case focused on the state's obligation to address concentrated poverty as part of its responsibility to provide a "sound basic education" statewide. Plaintiffs contended that the state is failing to meet its constitutional responsibility in the district not primarily through lack of funding, but rather by failing to do anything about the racial and economic isolation of students and by contributing to this isolation by changing housing policies to confine low-income units to certain areas. Plaintiffs also argued that school residency and nonresident tuition requirements preclude students in the district from attending schools that are more racially and economically integrated. Court records show that about 90% of the students in the Rochester schools are poor, about 80% are African-American or Hispanic, and all but 100 of the 2,494 units of public housing in Monroe County are in the city of Rochester. The court acknowledged "an abundance of terrible educational results" (*Paynter v. State of New York*, 2003, p. 6), including some of the lowest test scores and graduation rates in the state, as well as the links between concentrated poverty, racial isolation, and poor educational performance, but nevertheless argued that "if the state truly puts adequate resources into the classroom, it satisfies its constitutional promise ... even though student performance remains substandard" (p. 8).

In a lengthy dissent, Judge Smith argued that the majority interpreted the state's obligation far too narrowly:

> If students lack access to a sound basic education because of a high number of uncertified teachers, then it is the State's responsibility to remedy that problem. If the concentration of poor and minority students, assuming it is true, will necessarily result in schools that do not offer the opportunity of a sound basic education, even with adequate funding, then the State should remedy that problem. (pp. 40–41)

Judge Smith also took issue with the majority contention that plaintiffs were seeking a remedy that would trample on local control and potentially eliminate local school boards. "The alleged cause of the problem, the high concentration of poor and minority students, is not one that is beyond the power of the State to remedy" (p. 42), he argued, as plaintiffs asked only that the state "not draw district lines in a manner that encircles poor and minority students, and sets them up for failure" (p. 44).

A school reform effort with promise for poor children would require the political will, on the part of parents as well as judges and legislators, to push in a different direction—toward a shared commitment to the educational well-being of all young people and toward a sense of responsibility for all children, not just "ours." In her exploration of the role that "good schools" play in the decision making of parents wealthy enough to buy homes wherever they choose, Holme (2002) found that schools were these parents' main consideration. Nevertheless, few of the 42 parents Holme interviewed either researched schools themselves or sought factual information about schools from others. Rather, they acted on the basis of comments they heard other high-social-status (White and wealthy) parents make, and presumed that schools serving predominantly children from high-status families were "good" and that schools serving other children were not. When Holme asked why these parents opted not to look for a home in a particular school district or school attendance area, she heard a host of familiar but unsubstantiated rationalizations connecting academic achievement, motivation, and discipline, to race, ethnicity, and class.

This is the other side of ghetto schooling for ghettoized children: high-status schooling for well-to-do children. Flip sides of the same coin, this inequality in the provision of educational opportunity is rooted in a consciousness of "us" and "them" with a long social history. The public discourse on poverty for decades has reified a notion of social difference—the poor and the nonpoor, and among the poor, the "deserving" and the "undeserving" (Katz, 1989). This way of thinking finds a home in court judgments that rationalize inequalities and inadequacies in school funding as unfortunate, perhaps, but necessary to protect local control, in political foot dragging that allows legislatures to stall and underfund court-mandated school reforms, and in the No Child Left Behind Act, which threatens to create a two-tier school system: "deserving" schools (and students) that warrant public trust and funding, and "undeserving" schools (and students) that do not.

While society has made grandiose claims about all that education can do, its public schools for the most part have magnified social inequalities. Ensuring that public schooling does not further disadvantage already disadvantaged poor children, that at a minimum schooling does no harm, would be a major step forward. This would require more honesty about the significance of poverty in schooling, without either jumping to the conclusion that poor children are ineducable or handing over responsibility for solving massive social and economic problems to school principals and teachers, even if the handing off occurs through an inspirational rhetoric about the powers of education. An effort to do no harm also would require dedication to the attainable goal of providing educational opportunity, both equal and adequate, for all students, including and especially poor children who for so many years have done without.

I would like to be able to conclude this book with an "answer"—an easy, cost-free solution that would change the social and educational experience of poor children overnight. I cannot offer such a prescription, but also hope that readers will not jump to the unfounded conclusion that nothing can be done. It is possible in this wealthiest nation on earth to ensure that all children have enough to eat, a safe place to sleep, and an open door to a good school that welcomes them. We could come to regard all children as "our children" and put in place public policies designed to protect their well-being. But this cannot be accomplished either free of charge or with no change in existing structures that maintain privilege and advantage. As a society we need to move in a different direction, with a resolve that seeps through our social, political, legal, and educational institutions. I think of Curtis Hayes' reflection in the documentary film "Freedom on My Mind" (Field & Mulford, 1994) on the years he spent working in the Civil Rights Movement in the early 1960s:

> To hear of someone in danger and see people run to that danger as a hungry man would run to food—to give a hand, to give help. I still struggle to have that experience. I still look for that commitment to ideals greater than the individual that speak to the needs of the whole community of humanity.

Our society, like all others, was made by human hands. Nothing is foreordained or carved in stone. It is now entirely possible to establish a system of public schooling that bears witness to our highest ideals, including liberty, justice, equal opportunity, and giving a hand where it is needed for that reason alone: it's needed.

Appendix: Suggestions for Further Reading and Research

This book sweeps broadly to provide an overview of matters of poverty and schooling at a particular moment, the early years of the 21st century. The statistics cited to try to capture the big picture undoubtedly will change in the years ahead. For current information on poverty, I recommend these resources:

- For data on **child poverty** and related issues, the Children's Defense Fund [http://www.childrensdefense.org], a nonprofit child advocacy and educational organization, and the National Center for Children in Poverty [http://www.nccp.org], a research center at the Columbia University Mailman School of Public Health. See also the web sites of Save the Children [http://www.savethechildren.org], a nonprofit child-assistance organization that works in the United Staes as well as countries in the developing world, and, of course, the U.S. Census Bureau [http://www.census.gov/hhes/www/poverty.html].
- For up-to-date information on matters of **school funding**, ACCESS (Advocacy Center for Children's Educational Success with Standards) [http://www.accessednetwork.org], a project of the nonprofit Campaign for Fiscal Equity; the Council of the Great City Schools [http://www.cgcs.org], a coalition of 60 of the nation's largest urban school systems; and The Education Trust [http://www2.edtrust.org], a nonprofit organization dedicated to making schools and colleges work for all young people. Also of interest will be the annual *Quality Counts* report [http://www.edweek.org/sreports] published by *Education Week*, especially charts that rank and "grade" the states on the equity and adequacy of their school funding.

- For a deeper understanding of the **causes and consequences of poverty**, *Nickel and Dimed: On (Not) Getting By in America* (2001), by Barbara Ehrenreich; *The Undeserving Poor: From the War on Poverty to the War on Welfare* (1989), by Michael Katz; *Lives on the Edge: Single Mothers and their Children in the Other America* (1993), by Valerie Polakow; *Amazing Grace: The Lives of Children and the Conscience of a Nation* (1995), by Jonathan Kozol; and *When Work Disappears: The World of the New Urban Poor* (1996), by William Julius Wilson.
- To stay abreast of **current events in education**, the newspaper *Education Week* [http://www.edweek.org] and, for thoughtful commentary and a critical perspective on educational matters of the day, the newspaper *Rethinking Schools* [http://www.rethinkingschools.org].

References

Ahmad, N. (2002, October 9). Students walk, pay more as Minnesota schools cut costs. *Education Week, 22*(6), pp. 16–17.

Alliance to End Childhood Lead Poisoning. *Legal remedies.* Retrieved June 3, 2003, from *http://www.aeclp.org*

Alvarez, L. (1996, Oct. 9). Down from poverty: Mexico to Manhattan. *The New York Times,* pp. A1, B6–B7.

American Academy of Child & Adolescent Psychiatry (2002, January). *No. 64: Foster care.* Retrieved from *http://www.aacap.org/publications/factsfam/64.htm*

American Association of Colleges for Teacher Education (2004, January 9). *Member news bulletin: AACTE education policy clearinghouse.* Retrieved from *http://www.edpolicy.org*

American Society of Civil Engineers (2001). *Full report card for 2001.* Retrieved from *http://www.asce.org/reportcard/*

American Society of Civil Engineers (2003). *Report card for America's infrastructure: 2003 progress report.* Retrieved from *http://www.asce.org/reportcard/index.cfm*

America's Second Harvest (2003). *A profile of the working poor served by America's Second Harvest food banks.* Retrieved July 30, 2003, from *http://www.secondharvest.org*

Amrein, A. L., & Berliner, D. C. (2002a.) High-stakes testing, uncertainty, and student learning. *Education Policy Analysis Archives, 10*(18). Retrieved from *http://epaa.asu.edu/epaa/v10n18/*

Amrein, A. L., & Berliner, D. C. (2002b). *The impact of high-stakes tests on student academic performance: An analysis of NAEP results in states with high-stakes tests and ACT, SAT, and AP test results in states with high school graduation exams.* Report No. EPSL-0211-126. Tempe, AZ: Arizona State University, Education Policy Research Unit. Retrieved from *http://www.greatlakescenter.org/pub/H-S%20Impact%20final.pdf*

Andre, H. (Ed.). (1998). *Empirical poverty research in a comparative perspective.* Aldershot: Ashgate.

Anyon, J. (1997). *Ghetto schooling: A political economy of urban educational reform.* New York: Teachers College Press.

Archer, J. (2003, March 12). News in brief: A state capitals roundup. *Education Week, 22*(26), p. 21.

Arenson, K. W. (2003a, August 30). Public college tuition increases prompt concern, anguish and legislation. *The New York Times,* p. A10.

Arenson, K. W. (2003b, August 30). Scores on math Regents exam to be raised for thousands. *The New York Times,* p. B3.

As welfare hotels return, children recall what life inside was once like (1990, September 30). *The New York Times,* p. E5.

Barstow, D., & Bergman, L. (2003a, January 16). Two at hazardous foundry tell of events costing one his legs. *The New York Times.* Retrieved from *http://www.nytimes.com*

Barstow, D., & Bergman, L. (2003b, April 15). Pipe maker is fined over safety violations. *The New York Times.* Retrieved from *http://www.nytimes.com*

Belluck, P. (2000, May 18). Indian schools, long failing, press for money and quality. *The New York Times,* p. A1.

Berliner, D., & Biddle, B. (1995). *The manufactured crisis: Myths, fraud, and the attack on America's public schools.* Boston: Addison-Wesley.

Bernstein, N. (1997, May 4). Deletion of word in welfare bill opens foster care to big business. *The New York Times,* p. A1.

Bernstein, N. (2001a, March 25). Family is stranded at gates of New York shelter system. *The New York Times,* p. A1.

Bernstein, N. (2001b). *The lost children of Wilder: The epic struggle to change foster care.* New York: Pantheon.

Bernstein, N. (2002, July 29). Side effect of welfare law: The no-parent family. *The New York Times,* p. A1.

Blake, W. (2003). *Songs of innocence and songs of experience.* (Original work published 1789) Retrieved from The William Blake Archive, *http://www.blakearchive.org*

Board of Education of Oklahoma City v. Dowell, 498 U.S. 237 (1991).

Boo, K. (2001, April 9). After welfare. *The New Yorker,* pp. 92–107.

Books, S. (2000). Playing with numbers, playing with need: Schooling and the federal poverty line. *Educational Foundations, 14*(2), 5–20.

Books, S. (2000). Poverty and environmentally induced damage to children. In V. Polakow (Ed.), *The public assault on America's children: Poverty, violence, and juvenile injustice* (pp. 42–58). New York: Teachers College Press.

Books, S. (2001). High stakes in New York: From a "last chance, first chance" classroom. *Educational Foundations, 15*(4), 57–70.

Books, S. (2001). Saying poverty doesn't matter doesn't make it so. In J. Kincheloe & D. Weil (Eds.), *Schooling and Standards in the U.S.: An Encyclopedia* (pp. 245–258). Santa Barbara, CA: ABC-CLIO Publishers.

Books, S. (2002). Making poverty pay: Children and the 1996 welfare law. In G. S. Cannella & J. L. Kincheloe (Eds.), *Kidworld: Childhood studies, global perspectives, and education* (pp. 21–38). New York: Peter Lang.

Books, S. (2003). Funding accountability: States, courts, and public responsibility. *Educational Studies, 34*(3), 317–336.

Boshara, R. (2002, Sept. 29). Poverty is more than a matter of income. *The New York Times,* p. WK 13.

Boston Medical Center (2002, July 14). *Welfare sanctions associated with children's hospitalization and food insecurity.* Press release. Retrieved from *http://dcc2.bumc.bu.edu/csnappublic/press%20release*

Boushey, H., Brocht, C., Gundersen, B., & Bernstein, J. (2001). *Hardships in America: The real story of working families.* Washington, DC: Economic Policy Institute.

Bradbury, B., & Jantti, M. (2001). Child poverty across the industrialized world: Evidence from the Luxembourg Income Study. In K. Vleminckx & T. M. Smeeding, *Child well-being, child poverty, and child policy in modern nations: What do we know?* (pp. 11–31). Tonawanda, NY: University of Toronto Press.

Britzman, D. P. (2000). Teacher education in the confusion of our times. *Journal of Teacher Education, 51*(3), 200–205.

Brooks, J. L., Hair, E. C., & Zaslow, M. J. (2001, July). *Welfare reform's impact on adolescents: Early warning signs.* Research brief. Washington, DC: Child Trends.

Brown v. Board of Education of Topeka, 347 U.S. 483 (1954).

Brown II, 349 U.S. 294 (1955).

Browning, L. (2003, September 25). U.S. income gap widening, study says. *The New York Times.* Retrieved from *http://www.nytimes.com*

Bumiller, E. (2003, July 8). Bush seeks big changes in Head Start, drawing criticism from program's supporters. *The New York Times.* Retrieved from *http://www.nytimes.com*

Burch, K. (2001). A tale of two citizens: Asking the *Rodriguez* question in the 21st century. *Educational Studies, 32*(3), 264–278.

Campaign for Fiscal Equity v. State of New York, 719 N.Y.S. 2d 475 (2001). Can be retrieved from *http://www.cfequity.org/decision/html*

Campaign for Fiscal Equity v. State of New York, 744 N.Y.S. 2d 130 (2002).

Campaign for Fiscal Equity v. State of New York, 2003 NYSlip Op 15615 (2003).

Canada, G. (1995). *Fist stick knife gun: A personal history of violence in America.* Boston: Beacon Press.

Canedy, D. (2001, March 25). Troubling labor for Hispanics: "Girls most likely to drop out." *The New York Times,* p. A1.

Cardwell, D. (2002, August 17). Talks continue on jail as homeless shelter. *The New York Times,* p. B3.

Carter, S. C. (2000). *No excuses: Lessons from 21 high-performing high-poverty schools.* Washington, DC: The Heritage Foundation.

Center on Budget and Policy Priorities (2002, September 24). *Census data show increases in extent and severity of poverty and decline in household income.* Retrieved from *http://www.cbpp.org/9-24-02pov.htm*

Center for Children's Health and the Environment (1999, July 27). *Asthma hospitalization rates in poor NYC neighborhoods up to 5 times higher than the city average.* Press release. Retrieved from *http://www.childrenenvironment.org/press/1997-07-27.htm*

Center for Health, Environment, and Justice (2001, March). *Poisoned schools: Invisible threats, visible actions.* Report. Retrieved from *http://www.childproofing@chej.org*

Centers for Disease Control and Prevention (2003a). Childhood lead poisoning. Retrieved from *http://www.cdc.gov/nceh/lead/factsheets/childhoodlead.htm* Site reviewed March 6, 2003.

Centers for Disease Control and Prevention (2003b, January 31). *Second national report on human exposure to environmental chemicals.* NCEH Pub. No. 03-0022. Retrieved from *http://www.cdc.gov/exposurereport*

Century Foundation (2000). *Economic school integration.* Online dialogue series. Retrieved from *http://www.policyideas.org/Online_Dialogue/*

Chamberlin, J. G. (1999). *Upon whom we depend: The American poverty system.* New York: Peter Lang.

Chatterley, C. N., & Rouveral, A. J. (2000). *"I was content and not content": The story of Linda Lord and the closing of Penobscot Poultry.* Carbondale: Southern Illinois University Press.

Children's Defense Fund (2001a). *State of America's children: Yearbook 2001.* Washington, DC: Author.

Children's Defense Fund (2001b, April 10). *Statement by Marian Wright Edelman, founder and president of the Children's Defense Fund: Bush budget leaves children behind.* Press release. Retrieved from *http://www.childrensdefense.org*

Children's Defense Fund (2002a, December). *Basic facts on poverty.* Retrieved from *http://www.childrensdefense.org*

Children's Defense Fund (2002b, June 4). *Child poverty tops 50 percent in 14 U.S. counties.* Retrieved from *http://www.childrensdefense.org/release020604.php*

Children's Defense Fund (2002c). *The state of children in America's union: An action guide to Leave No Child Behind.* Retrieved from *http://www.childrensdefense.org*

Children's Defense Fund (2003, May 28). *Analysis: Number of black children in extreme poverty hits record high.* Washington, DC: Author.

Citro, C. F., & Michael, R. T. (1995). *Measuring poverty: A new approach.* Washington, DC: National Academy Press.

Clines, F. X. (2002, December 24). Life after welfare in the here and now of America's jammed shelters. *The New York Times.* Retrieved from *http://www.nytimes.com*

Cochran, K. T. (2000). Beyond school financing: Defining the constitutional right to an adequate education. *North Carolina Law Review, 78,* 399–476.

Cohn, D. (2003, May 18). D.C. pockets of poverty growing. *The Washington Post,* p. A1.

Coleman, J. (1966). *Equality of educational opportunity.* Washington, DC: U.S. Government Printing Office.

Comer, J. P. (1997). *Waiting for a miracle: Why schools can't solve our problems—and how we can.* New York: Dutton.

Connell, R. W. (1994). Poverty and education. *Harvard Educational Review, 64*(2), 125–149.

Connolly, C. (2002, May 15). Plan to ease lead testing regulations disavowed. *The Washington Post,* p. A25.

Cook J. T., Frank, D. A., Berkowitz, C., Black, M. M., Casey, P. H., Cutts, D. B., Meyers, A. F., Zaldivar, N., Skalicky, A., Levenson, S., & Heeren, T. (2002). Welfare reform and the health of young children. *Archives of Pediatrics and Adolescent Medicine, 156*(7), 678–684.

Corcoran, M. E., & Chaudry, A. (1997). The dynamics of childhood poverty. *Children and Poverty, 7*(2), 40–54.

Council of the Great City Schools (2001). *Beating the odds: A city-by-city analysis of the student performance and achievement gaps on state assessments.* Washington, DC: Author.

Council of the Great City Schools (2003, April). *Impact of budget cuts: What districts are doing to stay afloat.* Washington, DC: Author.

Court dismisses lawsuit brought against Department of Education under the "No Child Left Behind" Act (2003, June 26). Press release. New York City Law Department, Office of the Corporation Counsel. Retrieved from *http://www.nyc.gov/html/law/home.html*

Delisio, E. R. (2002, March 14). Grants help Baltimore schools aim high. *Education World.* Retrieved from *http://www.education-world.com/a_issues/issues287.shtml*

DeRolph v. State of Ohio, 728 N.E. 2d 993 (2000).

DeRolph v. State of Ohio (DeRolph III), 93 Ohio St.3d 309 (2001).

DeRolph v. State of Ohio (DeRolph IV), 97 Ohio St.3d 434, 2002-Ohio-6750 (2002).

Devine, J. A., & Wright, J. D. (1993). *The greatest of evils: Urban poverty and the American underclass.* New York: Aldine de Gruyter.

Dillon, S. (2003a, May 22). States are relaxing education standards to avoid sanctions from federal law. *The New York Times.* Retrieved from *http://www.nytimes.com*

Dillon, S. (2003b, May 24). Out of money, some school districts in Oregon end the year early. *The New York Times,* p. A13.

Dillon, S. (2003c, June 23). New federal law may leave many rural teachers behind. *The New York Times,* p. A1.

Dillon, S. (2003d, August 31). Outcry over Regents physics test, but officials in Albany won't budge. *The New York Times,* p. B1.

Dillon, S. (2003e, August 31). State cutbacks put schools and federal law to the test. *The New York Times,* p. A1.

Dodson, L. (1999). *Don't call us out of name: The untold lives of women and girls in poor America.* Boston: Beacon.

Drummond, S. E. (2000). Déjà vu: The state of school funding in Ohio after *DeRolph II. University of Cincinnati Law Review, 68,* 435–461.

Duncan, G. J., & Brooks-Gunn, J. (1997). *Consequences of growing up poor.* New York: Russell Sage Foundation.

Duncombe, W., & Yinger, J. (1998, March 16). How cost is linked to school performance. *The Wall Street Journal,* p. A23.

Eaton, S. E., Feldman, J., & Kirby, E. (1996). Still separate, still unequal: The limits of *Milliken II*'s monetary compensation. In G. Orfield & S. Eaton (Eds.), *Dismantling desegregation: The quiet reversal of Brown v. Board of Education* (pp. 143–178). New York: The New Press.

Edgewood Independent School District v. Kirby, 777 S.W. 2d 391 (Tex. 1989).

Education Funding Advisory Board. (2002, October). *Recommendations for systemic reform of funding for elementary and secondary education in Illinois.* Retrieved from *http://www.isbe.state.il.us/EFAB/PDFs/FinalReport1002.pdf*

Education reform left behind (2003, February 8). Editorial. *The New York Times,* p. A16.

Education Trust (1998). Good teaching matters: How well-qualified teachers can close the gap. *Thinking K–12, 3*(2), 1–7, 10.

Education Trust (2002, August). *The funding gap: Low-income and minority students receive fewer dollars.* Washington, DC: The Education Trust.

Education Week (2003). *Quality counts 2003: The great divide.* Retrieved from *http://www.edweek.org*

Ehrenreich, B. (2001). *Nickel and dimed: On (not) getting by in America.* New York: Metropolitan Books.

Ehrenreich, B., & Piven, F. F. (2002, May/June). Without a safety net. *Mother Jones, 27*(3), 34–41.

Enrich, P. (1995). Leaving equality behind: New directions in school finance reform. *Vanderbilt Law Review, 48,* 101–184.

Epstein, H. (2003, October 12). *The New York Times Magazine,* p. 12.

Excerpt from Bush statement announcing start of his education initiative (2001, January 24). *The New York Times,* p. A14.

Field, C., & Mulford, M. (Producer/Directors). (1994). *Freedom on my mind.* Film. San Francisco: California Newsreel.

Financial Oversight Panel for East St. Louis School District No. 189. (2002, September). *Annual Report to the State Superintendent.*

Fine, M., & Zane, N. (1991). Bein' wrapped too tight: When low-income women drop out of high school. *Women's Studies Quarterly, 19*(Spring/Summer), 80.

Firestone, D. (2003, September 14). Dizzying dive to red ink poses stark choices for Washington. *The New York Times,* p. A1.

Firestone, D., & Shanker, T. (2003, July 11). After the war: Price tag; war's cost brings democratic anger. *The New York Times,* p. A1.

Firestone, W. A., Goertz, M. E., & Natriello, G. (1997). *From cashbox to classroom: The struggle for fiscal reform and educational change in New Jersey.* New York: Teachers College Press.

Fletcher, M. A. (2003, January 2). States worry new law sets schools up to fail. *The Washington Post,* p. A1.

Frankenberg, E., Lee, C., & Orfield, G. (2003, January). *A multiracial society with segregated schools: Are we losing the dream?* Cambridge, MA: The Civil Rights Project, Harvard University.

Freedberg, L. (2003, January 6). Targeting school lunches. Editorial. *San Francisco Chronicle,* p. B6.

Freeman v. Pitts, 503 U.S. 467 (1992).

Freire, P. (1990). *Pedagogy of the oppressed.* New York: Continuum. (Original work published 1970)

Friedrich, M. J. (2000). Poor children subject to "environmental injustice." *The Journal of the American Medical Association, 283*(23), 3057.

Fulton, D. (2001, Sept. 24). Teach the children: Who decides? *The New York Times,* p. WK 14.

Gans, H. (1996). *The war against the poor: The underclass and antipoverty policy.* New York: Basic Books.

Garbarino, J. (1995). *Raising children in a socially toxic environment.* San Francisco: Jossey-Bass.

Gehring, J. (2002, Dec. 4). Court orders Arkansas to fix K–12 funding. *Education Week, 22*(14), 18, 20. Retrieved from *http://www.edweek.com*

Gewertz, C. (2001, January 10). California governor blames districts for poor conditions. *Education Week, 20*(6), p. 23.

Ghettoization. Companion text to "New York: A Documentary Film" (2001), directed by Ric Burns and produced by Steeplechase Films in association with WGBH Boston, Thirteen/WNET New York, and the New York Historical Society. Retrieved from *http://www.pbs.org/wnet/newyork/laic/episode6/topic4*

GI Forum v. Texas Education Agency, 87 F. Sup 2d 667 (W.D. Tex. 2000).

Goldberg, C. (1999, June 26). Many dentists won't fix poor children's bad teeth. *The New York Times,* p. A8.

Gratz, D. B. (2003, June 11). Leaving no child behind. *Education Week, 22*(40), 27, 36.

Greene, M. (1988). *The dialectic of freedom.* New York: Teachers College Press.

Greenhouse, S. (2000, August 6). Farm work by children tests labor laws. *The New York Times,* p. 12.

Greenhouse, S. (2002, December 20). U.S. jury cites unpaid work at Wal-Mart. *The New York Times,* p. A26.

Grissmer, D. W., Flanagan, A., Williamson, S., & Kawata, J. H. (Ed.). (2001). *Improving student achievement: What state NAEP test scores tell us.* Santa Monica, CA: Rand Corporation.

Gross, J. (2003, August 29). Free tutoring reaches only fraction of students. *The New York Times.* Retrieved from *http://www.nytimes.com*

Grossman, R. (1997, December 16). The East St. Louis challenge: Whose job is education? *Chicago Tribune,* pp. 1, 15.

Haberman, M. (1991, December). The pedagogy of poverty vs. good teaching. *Phi Delta Kappan, 73*(4), 290–2946

Haberman, M. (1994). Gentle teaching in a violent society. *Educational Horizons*(Spring), 131–135.

Haberman, M. (1995). *Star teachers of children in poverty.* West Lafayette, IN: Kappa Delta Pi.

Haberman, M. (2000). Urban schools: Day camps or custodial institutions? *Phi Delta Kappan, 82*(3), 203–208.

Halpern-Felsher, B. L., Connell, J. P., Spencer, M. B., Aber, J. L., Duncan, G. P., Clifford, E., Crichlow, W. E., Usinger, P. A., Cole, S. P., Allen, L., & Seidman, E. (1997). Neighborhood and family factors predicting educational risk and attainment in African American and white children and adolescents. In J. Brooks-Gunn, G. Duncan, & J. L. Aber (Eds.), *Neighborhood Poverty Volume I: Context and Consequences for Children* (pp. 146–173). New York: Russell Sage Foundation.

Hancock, L. (2002). *Hands to work: The stories of three families racing the welfare clock.* New York: William Morrow.

Harrington, M. (1962). *The other America.* New York: Macmillan.

Harvard Graduate School of Education (2001, January 31). *Dropouts concentrated in 35 cities, while federal data on dropouts underestimates problem.* Press release. Retrieved from *http://www.gse.harvard.edu/nv/features/conf01132001.html*

Hayden, J., & Cauthen, K. (Producers). (1998). *Children in America's schools.* Film. Columbia, SC: South Carolina ETV.

Heclo, H. (1994). Poverty politics. In S. H. Danzinger, G. D. Sandefur, & D. H. Weinberg (Eds.), *Confronting poverty: Prescriptions for change* (pp. 396–437). Cambridge: Harvard University Press.

Hendrie, C. (2003, October 29). Supreme Court declines Ohio school finance case. *Education Week, 23*(9), 23, 25.

Henriques, D. B., & Steinberg, J. (2001, May 20). Right answer, wrong score: Test flaws take toll. *The New York Times,* p. A1.

Herbert, B. (2001, September 3). In America; on the way to nowhere. *The New York Times.* Retrieved from *http://www.nytimes.com*

Herbert, B. (2003a, February 6). Young, jobless, hopeless. *The New York Times.* Retrieved from *http://www.nytimes.com*

Herbert, B. (2003b, May 1). Teaching kids a lesson. *The New York Times.* Retrieved from *http://www.nytimes.com*

Herbert, B. (2003c, June 2). The reverse Robin Hood. *The New York Times,* p. A17.

Herszenhorn, D. M. (2001, August 19). Rich states, poor cities and mighty suburbs. *The New York Times,* p. A39.

Herszenhorn, D. M. (2003, March 12). City begins informing parents about school-transfer rights. *The New York Times.* Retrieved from *http://www.nytimes.com*

Hewlett, S. A., & West, C. (1998). *The war against parents: What we can do for America's beleaguered moms and dads.* Boston: Houghton Mifflin.

Hicks-Bartlett, S. (2000). Between a rock and a hard place: The labyrinth of working and parenting in a poor community. In S. Danziger & A. C. Lin, *Coping with poverty: The social contexts of neighborhood, work, and family in the African-American community* (pp. 27–51). Ann Arbor: University of Michigan Press

Hilfiker, D. (2000). The limits of charity. *The Other Side Online, 36*(5). Retrieved from *http://www.theotherside.org/archive*

Hirsch, E. D. (2001). Overcoming the language gap. *American Educator, 25*(2), 4–7.

Hochschild, J. L., & Scovronick, N. (2003). *The American dream and the public schools.* New York : Oxford University Press.

Holahan, J., Dubay, L., & Kenney, G. M. (2003). Which children are still uninsured and why. *Future of Children, 13*(1), 55–79.

Holme, J. J. (2002). Buying homes, buying schools: School choice and the social construction of school quality. *Harvard Educational Review, 72*(2), 177–205.

Hunter, M. A. (2003). *State-by-state status of school finance litigations.* New York: Campaign for Fiscal Equity, Inc.

Hurst, M. D. (2003, January 8). Dental dilemma. *Education Week, 22*(16), 27–29.

Irons, P. (1988). *The courage of their convictions.* New York: The Free Press.

Jargowsky, P. A. (1997). *Poverty and place: ghettos, barrios, and the American city.* New York: Russell Sage Foundation.

Jerald, C. D. (1998, January 8). By the numbers: The urban picture. In *Quality Counts 1998.* Special report. *Education Week.* Retrieved from *http://www.edweek.com*

Johnston, D. C. (2003, January 26). Very richest's share of income grew even bigger, data show. *The New York Times.* Retrieved from *http://www.nytimes.com*

Jones, R. L., & Kaufman, L. (2003, May 31). New Jersey youths out of foster homes end up in detention. *The New York Times.* Retrieved from *http://www.nytimes.com*

Jordan, H. (2003). No child left unrecruited: Military recruiters have unprecedented access to our nation's students. *Rethinking Schools*(Spring), 9.

Kane, T. J., & Staiger, D. O. (2001, April). *Volatility in school test scores: Implications for school-based accountability systems.* Unpublished paper, Hoover Institution, Stanford University, Stanford, CA.

Kannapell, A. (1998, March 1). Moving (too slowly for some) to fight lead poisoning. *The New York Times,* p. NJ6.

Kantor, H., & Lowe, R. (1995). Class, race, and the emergence of federal education policy: From the New Deal to the Great Society. *Educational Researcher, 24*(3), 4–11, 21.

Karp, S. (1995). Money, schools, and courts: State by state battles against inequality. *Z Magazine*(December), 25–29.

Karp, S. (2003). Equity claims for NCLB don't pass the test. *Rethinking Schools*(Spring), 3–4.

Katz, M. B. (1987). *Reconstructing American education.* Cambridge: Harvard University Press.

Katz, M. B. (1989). *The undeserving poor: From the war on poverty to the war on welfare.* New York: Pantheon.

Katz, M. B. (1995). *Improving poor people: The welfare state, the "underclass," and urban schools as history.* Princeton: Princeton University Press.

Kaufman, L. (2002, August 31). City is ordered not to use jail as a shelter. *The New York Times,* p. B1.

Keller, B. (2003a, April 23). Mich. lists schools that miss progress mark. *Education Week, 22*(32), 18, 21.

Keller, B. (2003b, July 7). NEA takes stand against Bush education law. *Education Week, 22*(42). Retrieved from *http://www.educationweek.org*

Kennedy, M. M., Jung, R. K., & Orland, M. E. (January 1986). *Poverty, achievement and the distribution of compensatory education services.* Washington, DC: U.S. Government Printing Office.

Kingsley, G. T., & Pettit, K. L. (2003, May). Concentrated poverty: A change in course. *Neighborhood change in urban America (2).* Retrieved from *www.urban.org/nnip*

Kling, J., Liebman, J. B., & Katz, L. F. (2001). *Bullets don't got no name: Consequences of fear in the ghetto.* JCPR Working Paper 225. Chicago: Northwestern University/University of Chicago, Joint Center for Poverty Research.

Koch, K. (1999, December 10). Reforming school funding. *CQ Researcher, 9*(46), 1041–1063.

Kohn, A. (1999). *Punished by rewards: The trouble with gold stars, incentive plans, A's, praise, and other bribes.* Boston: Houghton Mifflin.

Kozol, J. (1991). *Savage inequalities: Children in America's schools.* New York: HarperCollins.

Kozol, J. (1995). *Amazing grace: The lives of children and the conscience of a nation.* New York: Crown.

Krugman, P. (2002, October 20). For richer. *The New York Times Magazine,* p. 62.

Landmark lawsuit on behalf of public school students demands basic education rights promised in state constitution (2000, May 17). *ACLU News.* Retrieved from *http://www.aclu.org/news/2000/n051700a.html*

Lake View v. Huckabee, No. 1992-5318 (Chancery Court, Pulaski County May 25, 2001).

Lareau, A. (1989). *Home advantage: Social class and parental intervention in elementary education.* New York: Falmer.

Leary, W. E. (1997, May 8). Cockroaches cited as big cause of asthma. *The New York Times,* p. A18.

Lee, V. E., & Burkam, D. T. (2002). *Inequality at the starting gate: Social background differences in achievement as children begin school.* Washington, DC: Economic Policy Institute.

Lessard, G., & Ku, L. (2003). Gaps in coverage for children in immigrant families. *Future of Children, 13*(1), 101–115.

Lewin, T. (2003, January 29). Uncle Sam wants student lists, and schools fret. *The New York Times,* p. B10.

Lewin, T., & Medina, J. (2003, August 1). To cut failure rate, schools shed students. *The New York Times,* p. A1.

Lewis E. v. Spagnolo, 83382 (Ill. S. Ct. 1999).

Livingston, D. R., & Livingston, S. M. (2002). Failing Georgia: The case against the ban on social promotion. *Education Policy Analysis Archives, 10*(49). Retrieved from *http://epaa.asu.edu/epaa/v10n49/*

Lu, H. (2003, July). *Low-income children in the United States.* Fact sheet. New York: National Center for Children in Poverty, Columbia University, Mailman School of Public Health.

Lunch, not just for eating (2002, January 13). *Education Life, The New York Times,* p. 15.

Lyter, D. M., Sills, M., & Oh, G. (2002, September). *Children in single-parents families living in poverty have fewer supports after welfare reform.* IWPR Publication # D451. Washington, DC: Institute for Women's Policy Research.

MacKinnon, D. (2002, May 21). The welfare Washington doesn't know. *The New York Times.* Retrieved from *http://www.nytimes.com*

Martin, J. R. (1992). *The schoolhome: Rethinking schools for changing families.* Cambridge: Harvard University Press.

Mathis, W. J. (2003). No Child Left Behind: Costs and benefits. *Phi Delta Kappan, 84*(9), 679.

Matsuda, M. (1997). Were you there: Witnessing welfare retreat. *University of San Francisco Law Review, 31,* 779–788.

McNeil, L. M. (2000). *Contradictions of school reform: Educational costs of standardized testing.* New York: Routledge.

McQuillan, P. (2003, June 18). Review of *Revolution at the margins: The impact of competition on urban school systems*, by Frederick Hess. *Education Review.* Retrieved from *http://edrev.asu/reviews/rev212.htm*

McUsic, M. S. (1999). The law's role in the distribution of education: The promises and pitfalls of school finance legislation. In J. P. Heubert (Ed.), *Law and school reform: Six strategies of promoting educational equity* (pp. 88–159). New Haven: Yale University Press.

Metropolis of poor children (2000, August 17). Editorial. *The New York Times.*

Milliken v. Bradley (Milliken I), 418 U.S. 717 (1974).

Milliken v. Bradley (Milliken II), 433 U.S. 267 (1977).

Miner, B. (2003). Privatizers' trojan horse: Bush's NCLB law funnels money to for-profits, churches, and voucher supporters. *Rethinking Schools*(Spring), 5.

Missouri v. Jenkins, 115 S. Ct. 2038 (1995).

Moore, M. (Producer & Director). (2002). *Bowling for Columbine.* Dog Eat Dog Films.

Moran, R. (2000). Sorting and reforming: High-stakes testing in the public schools. *Akron Law Review, 34*(1), 107–135.

Munger, F. (2001). *Laboring below the line: The new ethnography of poverty, low-wage work, and survival in the global economy.* New York: Russell Sage.

National Center for Post-Traumatic Stress Disorder. (2003). The effects of community violence on children and adolescents. Retrieved June 3, 2003, from *http://www.ncptsd.org/facts*

National Center for Public Policy and Higher Education. (2002, May). *Losing ground: A national status report on the affordability of American higher education.* Retrieved from *http://www.highereducation.org/reports/reports_center_2002.shtml*

National Coalition for the Homeless (2002, September). *Facts about homelessness.* Retrieved from *http://www.nationalhomeless.org*

National Commission on Children (1991). *Beyond rhetoric: A new American agenda for children and families.* Washington, DC: Author.

National Commission on Excellence in Education. (1983). *A nation at risk: The imperative for educational reform.* Washington, DC: U.S. Government Printing Office.

National Council of Teachers of Mathematics (2003). *Task force on mathematics teaching and learning in poor communities.* Retrieved from *http://www.nctm.org/about/committees/rac.tfpc/summary.htm*

National Low Income Housing Coalition (2002). *Out of reach 2002.* Retrieved from *http://www.nlihc.org/oor2002*

Natriello, G., McDill, E. L., & Pallas, A. M. (1990). *Schooling disadvantaged children: Racing against catastrophe.* New York: Teachers College Press.

Needleman, H. L., Riess, J. A., Tobin, M. J., Biesecker, G. E., & Greenhouse, J. B. (1996, February 7). Bone lead levels and delinquent behavior. *JAMA, 275*(5), 363–369.

New York Immigration Coalition and Advocates for Children (2002, June 18). *Report documents rising dropout rate for immigrant students still learning English.* Press release. Retrieved from *http://www.advocatesforchildren.org*

Noddings, N. (1992). *The challenge to care in schools: An alternative approach to education.* New York: Teachers College Press.

Nord, M., Kabbani, N., Tiehen, L., Andrews, M., Bickel, G., & Carlson, S. (2002, February). *Household food security in the United States, 2000.* Report No. 21. Washington, DC: U.S. Department of Agriculture, Food Assistance and Nutrition Research.

Oakes, J. (1985). *Keeping track: How schools structure inequality.* New Haven: Yale University Press.

O'Connor, S. (2001, May 26). When children relied on faith-based agencies. *The New York Times,* p. A13.

Olson, L. (2000, Sept. 27). High poverty among young makes schools' job harder. *Education Week, 20*(4), 40–41.

Olson, L. (2003a, February 19). States' plans likely to test ESEA pliancy. *Education Week, 22*(23), 1, 22, 23.

Olson, L. (2003b). All states get federal nod on key plans. *Education Week, 22*(41), 1, 20, 21.

Olson, L. (2003c). The great divide. *Quality Counts 2003. Education Week* special report, pp. 9–10, 13–14, 16, 18.

Orel, S. (2003). Left behind in Birmingham: 522 pushed-out students. In R. Cossett Lent & G. Pipkin (Eds.), *Silent no more: Voice of courage in Americans schools* (pp. 1–14). Portsmouth, NH: Heinemann.

Orenstein, P. (1994). *Schoolgirls: Young women, self esteem, and the confidence gap.* New York: Doubleday.

Orfield, G. (1996). Turning back to segregation. In G. Orfield & S. Eaton, *Dismantling desegregation: The quiet reversal of Brown v. Board of Education* (pp. 1–22). New York: The New Press.

Orfield, G. (1999). Conservative activists and the rush toward resegregation. In J. P. Heubert (Ed.), *Law and school reform: Six strategies for promoting educational equity* (pp. 39–87). New Haven: Yale University Press.

Orfield, G. (2001). Schools more separate: Consequences of a decade of resegregation. *Rethinking Schools Online, 16*(1). Retrieved from *http://www.rethinkingschools.org/archive/16_01/Seg161.shtml*

Orfield, M. (1997). *Metropolitics: A regional agenda for community and stability.* Washington, DC: Brookings Institution Press.

Orland, M. E. (1994). Demographics of disadvantage: Intensity of childhood poverty and its relationship to educational achievement. In J. I. Goodlad & P. Keating (Eds.), *Access to knowledge: The continuing agenda for our nation's schools* (pp. 43–58). New York: College Entrance Examination Board.

Orr, M., Stone, C. N., & Stumbo, C. (2000). *Concentrated poverty and educational achievement: Politics and possibility in the Baltimore region.* University of Maryland, Department of Government and Politics. Retrieved from *http://www.bsos.umd.edu/gvpt/stone/baltimore.html*

Park, J. (2003). School finance. *Education Week.* Retrieved from *http://www.edweek.com/context/topics*

Patterson, J. T. (2001). Brown v. Board of Education: *A civil rights milestone and its troubled legacy.* New York: Oxford University Press.

Payne, K. J., & Biddle, B. J. (1999). Poor school funding, child poverty, and mathematics achievement. *Educational Researcher, 28*(6), 4–13.

Payntor v. State of New York, 2003 NYSlip Op 15614.

Pear, R. (1995, March 25). House backs bill undoing decades of welfare policy. *The New York Times.* Retrieved from *http://www.nytimes.com*

Pear, R. (2003a, February 5). President's budget proposal: The poor; aid to poor faces tighter scrutiny. *The New York Times,* p. A1.

Pear, R. (2003b, February 11). Renters receiving U.S. aid to pay more under budget. *The New York Times,* p. A18.

Pear, R. (2003c, February 14). House endorses stricter work rules for poor. *The New York Times,* p. A25.

Perez-Pena (2003, May 1). Study finds asthma in 25% of children in central Harlem. *The New York Times,* p. A1.

Petronicolos, L., & New, W. S. (1999). Anti-immigrant legislation, social justice, and the right to equal educational opportunity. *American Educational Research Journal, 36*(3), 373–408.

Pew Environmental Health Commission (2000). Attack asthma: Why America needs a public health defense system to battle environmental threats. Retrieved from *http://healthyamericans.org/resources/files/asthma.pdf*

Piketty, T., & Saez, E. (2001). *Income inequality in the United States, 1913–1998.* NBER Working Paper No. 8467. Cambridge: National Bureau of Economic Research.

Plessy v. Ferguson, 163 U.S. 537 (1896).

Polakow, V. (1993). *Lives on the edge: Single mothers and their children in the other America.* Chicago: University of Chicago Press.

Polakow, V. (Ed.). (2000). *The public assault on America's children: Poverty, violence, and juvenile injustice.* New York: Teachers College Press.

Polakow, V. (2003). Homeless children and their families: The discards of the post-welfare era. In S. Books (Ed.), *Invisible children in the society and its schools* (2nd ed., pp. 89–100). Mahwah, NJ: Lawrence Erlbaum Associates.

Polakow-Suransky, S. (2001). Review of *Teacher with a heart: Reflections on Leonard Covello and community,* by Vito Perrone. *Educational Studies, 32*(3), 337–345.

Prince, C. D. (2002). Attracting well-qualified teachers to struggling schools. *American Educator*(Winter), 16–21, 50.

Proefriedt, W. A. (2001, July 11). Dead horses, buried assumptions. *Education Week, 20*(42), 48, 50–51.

Proefriedt, W. A. (2002, November 20). Other people's children. *Education Week, 22*(12), 33, 44.

Public colleges, broken promises (2002, May 5). Editorial. *The New York Times,* p. WK 14.

Public papers of the presidents of the United States: Lyndon B. Johnson, 1965. (1966). Vol. 1, entry 181, 412–414. Washington, DC: Government Printing Office.

Puma, M. J., Jones, C. C., Rock, D., & Fernandez, R. (1993). *Prospects: The congressionally mandated study of educational growth and opportunity.* Interim report. Washington, DC: U.S. Department of Education, Planning and Evaluation Service.

Purpel, D. E., & Shapiro, H. S. (1995). *Beyond liberation and excellence: Reconstructing the public discourse on education.* Westport, CT: Bergin & Garvey.

Rank, M. R. (1999). The racial injustice of poverty. *Journal of Law and Policy, 1*(95), 95–98.

Reid, K. S. (2003, March 19). School aid is casualty of Ohio's budget war. *Education Week, 22*(16), 13, 15. Retrieved from *http://www.edweek.com*

Reid, T. R. (2002, December 26). Seven states adopt four-day school week. *The Washington Post,* p. A3.

Rethinking Schools. (2003, Spring), *17*(3).

Reynolds, A. J., Temple, J. A., Robertson, D. L., & Mann, E. A. (2001). Long-term effects of an early childhood intervention on educational achievement and juvenile arrest. *Journal of the American Medical Association, 285,* 2339–2346.

Richard, A. (2001, September 26). Ohio governor wants finance case reopened. *Education Week, 21*(4), 24.

Richard, A. (2002, May 22). Broad effort to mix students by wealth under fire in N.C. *Education Week, 21* (37), pp. 1, 18, 19.

Richer, E., Savner, S., & Greenberg, M. (2001, November). *Frequently asked questions about working welfare leavers.* Center for Law and Social Policy report. Retrieved from *http://www.clasp.org/pubs/TANF/leaversFAQ.pdf*

Rimer, S. (2003, May 8). Cambridge schools try integration by income. *The New York Times.* Retrieved from *http://www.nytimes.com*

Robinson v. Cahill, 62 N.J. 473, 303 A. 2d 173 (1973).

Romano, L. (2002, December 29). Tulsa's desperate times and measures. *The Washington Post,* p. A3.

Rothenberg, D. (1998). *With these hands: The hidden world of migrant farmworkers today.* New York: Harcourt Brace.

Rothstein, R. (2000, October 4). Offering students a hand to move up. *The New York Times,* p. B13.

Rothstein, R. (2001, August 1). When there's simply not enough food for thought. *The New York Times,* p. B8.

Ruben, M. (2001). Suburbanization and urban poverty under neoliberalism. In J. Goode & J. Maskovsky (Eds.), *The new poverty studies: The ethnography of power, politics and impoverished people in the United States* (pp. 435–469). New York: NYU Press.

Ryan, J. E. (1999a). The influence of race in school finance reform. *Michigan Law Review, 98*(2), 432–481.

Ryan, J. E. (1999b). Schools, race, and money. *Yale Law Journal, 109*(2), 249–316.

Ryan, S. (2001, April 22). Overburdened students. *The New York Times,* p. 16.

Ryan, W. (1976). *Blaming the victim.* New York: Random House.

San Antonio Independent School District v. Rodriguez, 411 U.S. 1 (1973).

Sandham, J. L. (2000, May 24). California schools lack basics, suit alleges. *Education Week.* Retrieved from *http://www.educationweek.com*

Save the Children (2002, June). *America's forgotten children: Child poverty in rural America.* Retrieved from *http://www.savethechildren.org/americasforgotten.shtml*

Schemo, D. J. (2001, July 20). U.S. schools turn more segregated, a study finds. *The New York Times,* p. A14.

Schemo, D. J. (2002a, June 13) Education dept. says states have lax standards for teachers. *The New York Times,* p. A37.

Schemo, D. J. (2002b, December 2). Poor rural schools must strive to meet new federal rules. *The New York Times.* Retrieved from *http://www.nytimes.com*

Schemo, D. J. (2002c, December 10). Schools face new policy on transfers. *The New York Times,* p. A26.

Schemo, D. J. (2003a, February 5). The president's budget proposal: Education; critics say money for schools falls short of promises. *The New York Times.* Retrieved from *http://www.nytimes.com*

Schemo, D. J. (2003b, July 11). Questions on data cloud luster of Houston schools. *The New York Times.* Retrieved from *http://www.nytimes.com*

School district tries to force overhaul. (2004, January 4). *The New York Times,* p. 10.

School lunch "cheaters" (2003, January 23). Editorial. *San Francisco Chronicle,* p. A20.

School segregation on the rise despite growing diversity among school-aged children (2001, July 17). Press release. Harvard Graduate School of Education. Retrieved from *http://gseweb.harvard.edu/news/features/orfield07172001.html*

Schumacher, R., & Mezey, R. (2003, July 11). *Headed in the wrong direction: Why the House Head Start bill (H.R. 2210) is unlikely to make the program better.* Center for Law and Social Policy. Retrieved from *http://www.clasp.org/DMS/Documents/1057944079.98/view_html*

Sen, A. (1999). *Development as freedom.* New York: Knopf.

Sennett, R., & Cobb, J. (1993). *The hidden injuries of class.* New York: W. W. Norton.

Serrano v. Priest, 487 P.2d 1241 (Cal. 1971).

Sherman, A. (1997). *Poverty matters: The cost of child poverty in America.* Washington, DC: Children's Defense Fund.

Shirk, M., Bennett, N. G., & Aber, J. L. (1999). *Lives on the line: American families and the struggle to make ends meet.* Boulder, CO: Westview Press.

Sidel, R. (1986). *Women & children last: The plight of poor women in affluent America.* New York: Viking.

Silver, H., & Silver, P. (1991). *An educational war on poverty: American and British policy-making 1960–1980.* Cambridge, MA: Cambridge University Press.

Smiley, T. (2003, March 6). *Marian Wright Edelman on the Bush administration's plan to hand control of Head Start program to states.* Interview transcript. National Public Radio.

Steinberg, J., & Henriques, D. B. (2001, May 21). When a test fails the schools, careers and reputations suffer. *The New York Times,* p. A1.

Steinhauer, J. (2002, August 13). A jail becomes a shelter, and maybe a mayor's albatross. *The New York Times,* p. B1.

Sterngold, J. (1999, September 3). Bush would deny money to schools judged as failing. *The New York Times.* Retrieved from *http://www.nytimes.com*

Stewart, B. (2001, April 22). As garbage piles up, so do complaints. *The New York Times,* p. 37.

Sum, A., Khatiwada, I., Pond, N., & Trub'skyy, M. (2002, November). *Left behind in the labor market: Labor market problems of the nation's out-of-school, young adult populations.* Paper prepared for Alternative Schools Network, Chicago.

Swadener, B. B., & Lubeck, S. (1995). *Children and families "at promise": Deconstructing the discourse of risk.* Albany: State University of New York Press.

Taylor, W. (2000, Nov. 15). Standards, tests, and civil rights. *Education Week.* Retrieved from *http://www.educationweek.com*

Thernstrom, S., & Thernstrom, A. (1997). *America in black and white: One nation, indivisible.* New York: Simon & Schuster.

Threat to impoverished schools (1999, March 10). Editorial. *The New York Times.* Retrieved from *http://www.nytimes.com*

Tompkins, R. B. (2003, March 26). Leaving rural children behind. *Education Week, 22*(28), 30, 31, 44.

Toner, R., & Pear, R. (2003, April 28). Cutbacks imperil health coverage for states' poor. *The New York Times.* Retrieved from *http://www.nytimes.com*

Traub, J. (2000, January 16). What no school can do. *The New York Times Magazine,* pp. 52–57, 68, 81, 90–91.

Uchitelle, L. (2001a, February 18). By listening 3 economists show slums hurt the poor. *The New York Times,* p. BU 4.

Uchitelle, L. (2001b, May 26). How to define poverty? Let us count the ways. *The New York Times,* p. B7.

United Nations Children's Fund (2000a, June). *A league table of child poverty in rich nations.* Innocenti Report Card No. 1. Florence, Italy: Innocenti Research Centre.

United Nations Children's Fund (2000b). *The state of the world's children 2000.* New York: Author.

U.S. Conference of Mayors (2002, December). *A status report on hunger and homelessness in America's cities 2002: A 25-city survey.* Retrieved from *http://www.usmayors.org/uscm/hungersurvey/2002/onlinereport/HungerAndHomelessReport2002.pdf*

U.S. Department of Education (1999). *Promising results, continuing challenges: The final report of the national assessment of Title I. Executive summary.* Washington, DC: U.S. Department of Education, Office of the Under Secretary, Planning and Evaluation Service.

U.S. Department of Education (2001, January). *High standards for all students: A report from the national assessment of Title I on progress and challenges since the 1994 reauthorization.* Washington, DC: U.S. Department of Education, Office of the Under Secretary, Planning and Evaluation Service.

U.S. Department of Health and Human Services (2000). *Oral health in America: A report of the surgeon general.* Rockville, MD: U.S. Department of Health and Human Services, National Institute of Dental and Craniofacial Research, National Institutes of Health.

U.S. General Accounting Office (1996, June). *School facilities: America's schools report differing conditions.* GAO/HEHS-96-103.

U.S. General Accounting Office. (1997, February). *School finance: State efforts to reduce funding gaps between poor and wealthy districts.* GAO/HEHS-97-31.

U.S. General Accounting Office. (1999). *Lead poisoning: Federal health care programs are not effectively reaching at-risk children.* GAO/HEHS-99-18.

U.S. General Accounting Office. (2003a, May). *Child care: Recent state policy changes affecting the availability of assistance for low-income families.* GAO-03-588.

U.S. General Accounting Office (2003b, May). *Title I: Characteristics of tests will influence expenses; information sharing may help states realize efficiencies.* GAO-03-389.

Valenzuela, A. (1999). *Subtractive schooling: U.S.-Mexican youth and the politics of caring.* Albany: SUNY Press.

Vorrasi, J. A., & Garbarino, J. (2000). In V. Polakow (Ed.), *The public assault on America's children: Poverty, violence, and juvenile injustice* (pp. 59–77). New York: Teachers College Press.

Walker, R. (1998). Rethinking poverty in a dynamic perspective. In Andreß, H. (Ed.), *Empirical poverty research in a comparative perspective* (pp. 29–49). Aldershot: Ashgate.

Walsh, M. W. (2003, April 25). I.R.S. tightening rules for low-income tax credit. *The New York Times.* Retrieved from *http://www.nytimes.com*

Wayne, A. J. (2002, June 13). Teacher inequality: New evidence on disparities in teachers' academic skills. *Educational Policy Analysis Archives, 10*(30). Retrieved from *http://epaa.asu.edu/epaa/v10n30*

Weissbourd, R. (1996). *What really hurts America's children and what we can do about it.* Reading, MA: Addison-Wesley.

Wexler, R. (1990). *Wounded innocents: The real victims of the war against child abuse.* Buffalo, NY: Prometheus.

White, K. A. (1999, Oct. 20). L. A. board names CEO with broad powers. *Education Week,* p. 3.

Williams, B. (2001). What's debt got to do with it? In J. Goode & J. Maskovsky (Eds.), *The new poverty studies: The ethnography of power, politics and impoverished people in the United States* (pp. 79–102). New York: NYU Press.

Williams, J. (1998). *Thurgood Marshall: American revolutionary.* New York: Random House.

Williams et al. v. State of California, 2000. Complaint retrieved from *http://www.aclunc.org /students/ca-school-complaint.html*

Wilson, W. J. (1996). *When work disappears: The world of the new urban poor.* New York: Knopf.

Wilson, W. J. (2003, June 16). There goes the neighborhood. *The New York Times,* p. A19.

Winerip, M. (2003a, March 19). A pervasive dismay on a Bush school law. *The New York Times.* Retrieved from *http://www.nytimes.com*

Winerip, M. (2003b, September 3). A star! A failure! Or caught between unmeshed yardsticks? *The New York Times,* p. B7.

Winerip, M. (2003c, September 10). No Child Left Behind law leaves no room for some. *The New York Times.* Retrieved from *http://www.nytimes.com*

Winter, G. (2002, October 19). Poorer boroughs' students get smaller slice of aid. *The New York Times,* p. A1.

Winter, G. (2003, July 23). California will wait until 2006 to require high school graduates to pass exit exam. *The New York Times,* p. A16.

Wong, D. S. (1996, March 2). Welfare bill's aim: ID fathers; payment for child could be withheld. *Boston Globe,* p. B1.

Wong, E. (2000, August 13). Poorest schools lack teachers and computers. *The New York Times,* p. A16.

Zehr, M. A. (2003, May 28). Ohio court declares end to *DeRolph* school funding case. *Education Week, 22*(38), 15.

Author Index

A

B

C

D

E

F

G

H

I

J

K

Subject Index

G

H

I

J

K

L

M

N

T

U

V

W